SPECTRUM®

Grade 2

Published by Spectrum®
an imprint of Carson-Dellosa Publishing
Greensboro, NC

Spectrum®
An imprint of Carson-Dellosa Publishing LLC
P.O. Box 35665
Greensboro, NC 27425 USA

Printed in the USA • All rights reserved.   ISBN 978-1-4838-1626-5

01-023157897

Table of Contents Grade 2

Math

Language Arts

Reading

SPECTRUM®

Math

Chapter 1

NAME _____

Lesson 1.1 Grouping Objects

Write an equation to match each array.

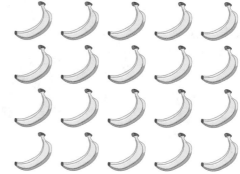

$$\underline{3} + \underline{3} = \underline{6}$$

$$\underline{5} + \underline{5} + \underline{5} + \underline{5} = \underline{20}$$

$$\underline{\quad} + \underline{\quad} + \underline{\quad} = \underline{\quad}$$

$$\underline{\quad} + \underline{\quad} + \underline{\quad} + \underline{\quad} + \underline{\quad} = \underline{\quad}$$

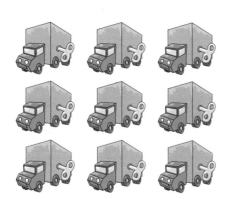

$$\underline{\quad} + \underline{\quad} + \underline{\quad} = \underline{\quad}$$

$$\underline{\quad} + \underline{\quad} = \underline{\quad}$$

Lesson 1.1 Grouping Objects

Write an equation to match each array.

_____ + _____ = _____

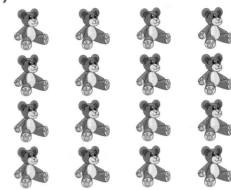

_____ + _____ + _____ + _____ = _____

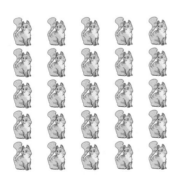

_____ + _____ = _____

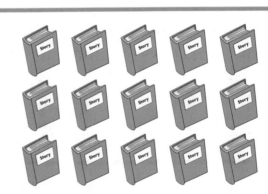

_____ + _____ + _____ = _____

_____ + _____ + _____ + _____ + _____

= _____

_____ + _____ = _____

Lesson 1.2 Skip Counting

Count by 2. Write the missing numbers.

2,   4,   6,   _8_,   10,   12,   ____

Count by 5. Write the missing numbers.

5,   10,   _15_,   ____,   25,   ____,   ____

Count by 10. Write the missing numbers.

 _40_   ____   ____

Count by 2. Write the missing numbers.

12,   _14_,   ____,   18,   20,   ____,   24,   26,   28

Count by 5. Write the missing numbers.

15,   _20_,   25,   ____,   ____,   40,   45,   50

____,   60,   ____,   70,   ____,   ____,   85

Count backward by 10. Write the missing numbers.

100,   90,   _80_,   70, ____,   50,   ____,   ____,   20,   10

Lesson 1.3 Skip Counting with Money

A penny is 1¢

A nickel is 5¢

A dime is 10¢

Count pennies by 2. Write the missing numbers.

2¢,   4¢,   6¢,   __8__ ¢,   _____ ¢,   _____ ¢

Count by 2. Start at 80¢. Write the missing numbers.

80¢,   82¢,   __84__ ¢,   86¢,   _____ ¢,   _____ ¢

Count by 5. Write the missing numbers.

5¢,   __10__ ¢,   15¢,   _____ ¢,   25¢,   _____ ¢

Lesson 1.3 Skip Counting with Money

Count by 5. Start at 50¢.

50¢,   ___5_5__ ¢,   60¢,   _____ ¢,   70¢,   _____ ¢

Count by 10.

10¢,   ___20__ ¢,   30¢,   _____ ¢,   _____ ¢,   60¢,

70¢,   _____ ¢,   _____ ¢,   100¢

Count backward by 10. Start at 100¢.

100¢,   90¢,   __80__ ¢,   70¢,   _____ ¢,   50¢,

_____ ¢,   _____ ¢,   _____ ¢,   10¢

Lesson 1.4 Odd or Even?

even

$3 + 3 = 6$

odd

odd

even

$1 + 1 = 2$

How many fish? __8__

Odd or even? __even__

__4__ + __4__ = 8

How many birds? _____

Odd or even? _____

Lesson 1.4 Odd or Even?

Circle the groups that are odd.

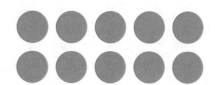

Tell how many. Label odd or even. Write an equation.

__8__ dolls ___even___

__4__ + __4__ = 8

_____ cars

_____

_____ jets

_____

___ bears _____

___ + ___ = ___

	1 ← addend → 2	
	+3 ← addend → +0	
	4 ← sum → 2	

Add.

$$\begin{array}{r} 2 \\ +3 \\ \hline 5 \end{array} \qquad \begin{array}{r} 2 \\ +2 \\ \hline \end{array} \qquad \begin{array}{r} 1 \\ +4 \\ \hline \end{array} \qquad \begin{array}{r} 4 \\ +0 \\ \hline \end{array} \qquad \begin{array}{r} 0 \\ +1 \\ \hline \end{array} \qquad \begin{array}{r} 2 \\ +1 \\ \hline \end{array}$$

$$\begin{array}{r} 0 \\ +2 \\ \hline \end{array} \qquad \begin{array}{r} 1 \\ +1 \\ \hline \end{array} \qquad \begin{array}{r} 5 \\ +0 \\ \hline \end{array} \qquad \begin{array}{r} 1 \\ +2 \\ \hline \end{array} \qquad \begin{array}{r} 1 \\ +3 \\ \hline \end{array} \qquad \begin{array}{r} 3 \\ +0 \\ \hline \end{array}$$

$$\begin{array}{r} 3 \\ +1 \\ \hline \end{array} \qquad \begin{array}{r} 0 \\ +0 \\ \hline \end{array} \qquad \begin{array}{r} 3 \\ +2 \\ \hline \end{array} \qquad \begin{array}{r} 0 \\ +4 \\ \hline \end{array} \qquad \begin{array}{r} 2 \\ +2 \\ \hline \end{array} \qquad \begin{array}{r} 0 \\ +2 \\ \hline \end{array}$$

$$\begin{array}{r} 1 \\ +0 \\ \hline \end{array} \qquad \begin{array}{r} 4 \\ +1 \\ \hline \end{array} \qquad \begin{array}{r} 0 \\ +3 \\ \hline \end{array} \qquad \begin{array}{r} 1 \\ +3 \\ \hline \end{array} \qquad \begin{array}{r} 2 \\ +3 \\ \hline \end{array} \qquad \begin{array}{r} 2 \\ +0 \\ \hline \end{array}$$

$$\begin{array}{r} 0 \\ +0 \\ \hline \end{array} \qquad \begin{array}{r} 1 \\ +1 \\ \hline \end{array} \qquad \begin{array}{r} 0 \\ +5 \\ \hline \end{array} \qquad \begin{array}{r} 2 \\ +1 \\ \hline \end{array} \qquad \begin{array}{r} 3 \\ +1 \\ \hline \end{array} \qquad \begin{array}{r} 1 \\ +4 \\ \hline \end{array}$$

Lesson 2.2 Subtracting from 0 through 5

There are 4 fish. 2 swim away.
How many fish are left?

$$\begin{array}{r} 4 \\ -2 \\ \hline 2 \end{array} \leftarrow \text{difference}$$

Subtract.

4 −1 = 3	3 −3	1 −1	5 −4	3 −0	5 −2
2 −2	1 −0	5 −5	4 −3	5 −3	4 −0
5 −1	4 −2	2 −0	0 −0	3 −1	4 −1
2 −1	5 −0	4 −4	5 −2	2 −2	3 −3
3 −2	4 −1	5 −4	4 −2	3 −0	5 −1

Lesson 2.3 Adding to 6, 7, and 8

 5
       +3
       8 ← sum → 7

1
$+6$

Add.

0	4	1	3	6	8
+6	+4	+6	+4	+2	+0
6					

3	5	7	2	5	7
+3	+1	+0	+4	+3	+1

4	2	1	6	4	6
+3	+5	+7	+1	+2	+0

0	5	5	2	1	0
+8	+3	+2	+6	+5	+7

3	4	3	2	3	1
+5	+4	+4	+4	+3	+6

Lesson 2.4 Subtracting from 6, 7, and 8

There are 7 balls.

5 are baseballs.

How many are not baseballs?

$$
\begin{array}{r} 7 \\ -5 \\ \hline 2 \end{array}
$$

Subtract.

$\begin{array}{r} 8 \\ -4 \\ \hline \end{array}$	$\begin{array}{r} 7 \\ -1 \\ \hline \end{array}$	$\begin{array}{r} 6 \\ -3 \\ \hline \end{array}$	$\begin{array}{r} 7 \\ -3 \\ \hline \end{array}$	$\begin{array}{r} 8 \\ -5 \\ \hline \end{array}$	$\begin{array}{r} 6 \\ -2 \\ \hline \end{array}$
$\begin{array}{r} 7 \\ -0 \\ \hline \end{array}$	$\begin{array}{r} 8 \\ -7 \\ \hline \end{array}$	$\begin{array}{r} 6 \\ -4 \\ \hline \end{array}$	$\begin{array}{r} 7 \\ -7 \\ \hline \end{array}$	$\begin{array}{r} 8 \\ -3 \\ \hline \end{array}$	$\begin{array}{r} 6 \\ -6 \\ \hline \end{array}$
$\begin{array}{r} 6 \\ -1 \\ \hline \end{array}$	$\begin{array}{r} 8 \\ -2 \\ \hline \end{array}$	$\begin{array}{r} 7 \\ -4 \\ \hline \end{array}$	$\begin{array}{r} 6 \\ -5 \\ \hline \end{array}$	$\begin{array}{r} 8 \\ -6 \\ \hline \end{array}$	$\begin{array}{r} 7 \\ -5 \\ \hline \end{array}$
$\begin{array}{r} 8 \\ -8 \\ \hline \end{array}$	$\begin{array}{r} 6 \\ -0 \\ \hline \end{array}$	$\begin{array}{r} 7 \\ -2 \\ \hline \end{array}$	$\begin{array}{r} 8 \\ -1 \\ \hline \end{array}$	$\begin{array}{r} 8 \\ -0 \\ \hline \end{array}$	$\begin{array}{r} 7 \\ -6 \\ \hline \end{array}$
$\begin{array}{r} 6 \\ -2 \\ \hline \end{array}$	$\begin{array}{r} 8 \\ -3 \\ \hline \end{array}$	$\begin{array}{r} 8 \\ -4 \\ \hline \end{array}$	$\begin{array}{r} 7 \\ -3 \\ \hline \end{array}$	$\begin{array}{r} 7 \\ -7 \\ \hline \end{array}$	$\begin{array}{r} 6 \\ -3 \\ \hline \end{array}$

Lesson 2.5 Adding to 9 and 10

   6   5

+3   +5

9 ⟵ sum ⟶ 10

Add.

8 +1	2 +8	4 +6	3 +6	7 +3	5 +4
7 +2	9 +0	8 +2	5 +5	9 +1	0 +9
6 +3	1 +8	3 +6	4 +5	2 +7	6 +4
5 +4	1 +9	7 +3	3 +7	0 +9	8 +1
7 +2	5 +5	9 +1	6 +4	2 +8	4 +5

Lesson 2.6 Subtracting from 9 and 10

Dani has 10 postage stamps.

 10

Felix has 6 postage stamps. −6

How many more stamps does Dani have?   4 ← difference

Subtract.

9	10	9	10	10	9
−6	− 5	−3	− 4	− 9	−7

10	9	9	10	9	10
− 1	−8	−5	− 8	−1	− 6

9	9	10	9	10	10
−0	−4	− 7	−2	− 3	− 0

9	10	9	10	10	9
−9	− 2	−3	− 9	− 1	−5

9	10	9	9	10	10
−8	− 5	−1	−7	− 8	− 3

Lesson 2.7 Adding to 11, 12, and 13

$$8 + 4 = 10 + 2 = \underline{12}$$

$$6 + 7 = 10 + 3 = \underline{13}$$

Add.

3 +9	4 +7	7 +6	9 +2	4 +8	6 +5
6 +6	9 +4	5 +7	9 +3	7 +4	5 +8
5 +6	8 +4	3 +8	6 +7	2 +9	4 +9
8 +5	8 +3	7 +5	9 +3	7 +6	6 +5
9 +2	5 +7	6 +6	5 +8	9 +4	3 +8

Lesson 2.8 Subtracting from 11, 12, and 13

13 = 1 ten 3 ones

 　Cross out to solve.

$$\begin{array}{r} 13 \\ -5 \\ \hline 8 \end{array}$$

12 = 1 ten 2 ones

Cross out to solve.

$$\begin{array}{r} 12 \\ -7 \\ \hline 5 \end{array}$$

Subtract.

$\begin{array}{r} 12 \\ -\ 4 \\ \hline \end{array}$	$\begin{array}{r} 11 \\ -\ 9 \\ \hline \end{array}$	$\begin{array}{r} 13 \\ -\ 9 \\ \hline \end{array}$	$\begin{array}{r} 12 \\ -\ 5 \\ \hline \end{array}$	$\begin{array}{r} 13 \\ -\ 4 \\ \hline \end{array}$	$\begin{array}{r} 11 \\ -\ 6 \\ \hline \end{array}$
$\begin{array}{r} 11 \\ -\ 8 \\ \hline \end{array}$	$\begin{array}{r} 13 \\ -\ 6 \\ \hline \end{array}$	$\begin{array}{r} 13 \\ -\ 8 \\ \hline \end{array}$	$\begin{array}{r} 12 \\ -\ 3 \\ \hline \end{array}$	$\begin{array}{r} 11 \\ -\ 5 \\ \hline \end{array}$	$\begin{array}{r} 12 \\ -\ 6 \\ \hline \end{array}$
$\begin{array}{r} 13 \\ -\ 4 \\ \hline \end{array}$	$\begin{array}{r} 11 \\ -\ 7 \\ \hline \end{array}$	$\begin{array}{r} 12 \\ -\ 9 \\ \hline \end{array}$	$\begin{array}{r} 12 \\ -\ 4 \\ \hline \end{array}$	$\begin{array}{r} 13 \\ -\ 7 \\ \hline \end{array}$	$\begin{array}{r} 11 \\ -\ 3 \\ \hline \end{array}$
$\begin{array}{r} 12 \\ -\ 5 \\ \hline \end{array}$	$\begin{array}{r} 13 \\ -\ 5 \\ \hline \end{array}$	$\begin{array}{r} 12 \\ -\ 8 \\ \hline \end{array}$	$\begin{array}{r} 11 \\ -\ 5 \\ \hline \end{array}$	$\begin{array}{r} 11 \\ -\ 4 \\ \hline \end{array}$	$\begin{array}{r} 13 \\ -\ 9 \\ \hline \end{array}$
$\begin{array}{r} 11 \\ -\ 2 \\ \hline \end{array}$	$\begin{array}{r} 13 \\ -\ 6 \\ \hline \end{array}$	$\begin{array}{r} 11 \\ -\ 8 \\ \hline \end{array}$	$\begin{array}{r} 12 \\ -\ 3 \\ \hline \end{array}$	$\begin{array}{r} 12 \\ -\ 7 \\ \hline \end{array}$	$\begin{array}{r} 11 \\ -\ 6 \\ \hline \end{array}$

Lesson 2.9 Adding to 14, 15, and 16

7 🐟🐟🐟🐟🐟🐟🐟   🐟🐟🐟🐟🐟🐟🐟🐟🐟🐟 10

+8 🐟🐟🐟🐟🐟🐟🐟🐟 =   🐟🐟🐟🐟🐟 +5

15   15

Add.

9	4	8	5	7	2
+5	+8	+8	+8	+7	+9

4	5	9	9	6	7
+7	+9	+4	+7	+6	+9

6	8	3	8	8	6
+8	+7	+9	+3	+6	+7

6	7	9	7	9	7
+9	+5	+3	+4	+6	+8

7	9	5	7	9	6
+6	+5	+6	+9	+2	+8

Lesson 2.10 Subtracting from 14, 15, and 16

	Think:		Cross out to solve.

16
−9
‾‾
7

Think:
16 = 1 ten 6 ones

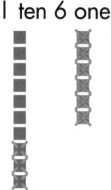

15
−6
‾‾
9

Cross out to solve.
15 = 1 ten 5 ones

Subtract.

14 − 9	15 − 8	13 − 8	11 − 3	14 − 7	12 − 8
11 − 6	16 − 7	14 − 8	12 − 5	13 − 4	11 − 5
14 − 5	13 − 6	15 − 7	11 − 9	12 − 6	14 − 6
13 − 9	12 − 9	15 − 9	16 − 8	11 − 2	15 − 6
11 − 4	16 − 9	12 − 7	13 − 5	14 − 9	14 − 7

Lesson 2.11 Adding to 17, 18, 19, and 20

$$\begin{array}{r} 9 \\ +8 \\ \hline 17 \end{array}$$

⚽⚽⚽⚽⚽⚽⚽⚽⚽
⚽⚽⚽⚽⚽⚽⚽⚽

$=$

$$\begin{array}{r} 10 \\ +7 \\ \hline 17 \end{array}$$

Add.

$\begin{array}{r}9\\+9\\\hline\end{array}$	$\begin{array}{r}8\\+9\\\hline\end{array}$	$\begin{array}{r}9\\+7\\\hline\end{array}$	$\begin{array}{r}5\\+8\\\hline\end{array}$	$\begin{array}{r}10\\+9\\\hline\end{array}$	$\begin{array}{r}3\\+9\\\hline\end{array}$
$\begin{array}{r}5\\+9\\\hline\end{array}$	$\begin{array}{r}12\\+8\\\hline\end{array}$	$\begin{array}{r}6\\+9\\\hline\end{array}$	$\begin{array}{r}8\\+4\\\hline\end{array}$	$\begin{array}{r}8\\+7\\\hline\end{array}$	$\begin{array}{r}9\\+8\\\hline\end{array}$
$\begin{array}{r}8\\+9\\\hline\end{array}$	$\begin{array}{r}7\\+7\\\hline\end{array}$	$\begin{array}{r}5\\+7\\\hline\end{array}$	$\begin{array}{r}9\\+4\\\hline\end{array}$	$\begin{array}{r}6\\+6\\\hline\end{array}$	$\begin{array}{r}8\\+6\\\hline\end{array}$
$\begin{array}{r}13\\+6\\\hline\end{array}$	$\begin{array}{r}8\\+5\\\hline\end{array}$	$\begin{array}{r}9\\+9\\\hline\end{array}$	$\begin{array}{r}7\\+8\\\hline\end{array}$	$\begin{array}{r}7\\+5\\\hline\end{array}$	$\begin{array}{r}17\\+3\\\hline\end{array}$
$\begin{array}{r}15\\+5\\\hline\end{array}$	$\begin{array}{r}9\\+5\\\hline\end{array}$	$\begin{array}{r}7\\+6\\\hline\end{array}$	$\begin{array}{r}9\\+8\\\hline\end{array}$	$\begin{array}{r}8\\+8\\\hline\end{array}$	$\begin{array}{r}12\\+7\\\hline\end{array}$

Lesson 2.12 Subtracting from 17, 18, 19 , and 20

$$\begin{array}{r} 17 \\ -\ 9 \\ \hline 8 \end{array}$$

Subtract.

18 − 9	16 − 8	13 − 7	17 − 9	15 − 9	20 − 9
12 − 9	17 − 8	14 − 6	13 − 8	16 − 9	12 − 6
15 − 7	14 − 8	13 − 5	19 − 7	12 − 7	18 − 9
17 − 9	16 − 7	14 − 9	13 − 9	19 − 3	15 − 8
20 − 5	15 − 6	17 − 8	12 − 8	14 − 7	20 −10

Lesson 2.13 Problem Solving

Solve each problem.

Steve has 7 fish.

Ramon has 13 fish.

How many more fish does Ramon have? __6__

$$\begin{array}{r} 13 \\ -\ 7 \\ \hline 6 \end{array}$$

Yolanda has 8 teddy bears.

Maria has 6 teddy bears.

How many do they have in all? _____

Gina bakes 15 cupcakes.

Her friends eat 7.

How many cupcakes are left? _____

6 students were in the classroom.

Now, there are 9 students in the classroom.

How many students came in? _____

$6 + \underline{\qquad} = 9$

Mark has 18 toy cars.

He gives 9 away.

How many cars does he have left? _____

Chapter 3

NAME _____

Lesson 3.1 Adding 2-Digit Numbers

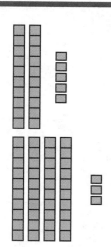

First add ones. Then, add tens.

$$
\begin{array}{r} 25 \\ +43 \\ \hline \end{array}
\qquad
\begin{array}{r} 25 \\ +43 \\ \hline 8 \end{array}
\qquad
\begin{array}{r} 25 \\ +43 \\ \hline \text{sum} \rightarrow 68 \end{array}
$$

Add.

53 +11 64	36 +43	74 + 5	26 +61	40 +34
25 +51	44 + 4	15 +72	82 +12	66 +22
31 +60	57 +32	91 + 7	46 +23	52 +37
17 +70	28 +41	82 + 3	65 +14	35 +24
84 +11	27 +50	18 +80	38 +21	33 +20

Lesson 3.2 Subtracting 2-Digit Numbers

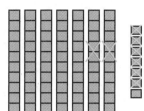

	First, subtract the ones.	Then, subtract the tens.
77 −26	77 −26 1	77 −26 51

Subtract.

49 −39 10	87 − 6 81	36 −24	54 −40	68 −16

79 −63	78 −25	42 −12	19 − 7	26 −11

59 −38	28 −14	95 −62	74 −50	67 −41

92 −81	35 − 5	77 −17	82 −51	86 −64

58 −53	75 −61	47 −37	89 −27	65 −60

NAME _____

Lesson 3.3 Problem Solving

SHOW YOUR WORK

Solve each problem.

Ms. Willis has 28 .

Mr. Sanchez borrows 10 .

How many does Ms. Willis have left? 18

$$\begin{array}{r} 28 \\ -10 \\ \hline 18 \end{array}$$

The first-grade class has 32 .

The second-grade class has 30 .

How many more does the first-grade class have? _____

The art room has 65 ✎.

Students are using 22 ✎.

How many ✎ are not being used? _____

Students had 44 🥛 at breakfast.

They had 59 🥛 at lunch. How many

more 🥛 did students have at lunch? _____

The library has 37 about computers. 37 − 12 = _____

12 of the have been borrowed. How

many about computers are still in the library? _____

Lesson 3.4 Adding Three Numbers

	Add the ones.	Add the tens.
23	23	23
44	44	44
+12	+12	+12
	9	79

Add.

13	62	44	16	22
50	11	23	40	32
+ 6	+15	+20	+12	+42
69				

22	30	71	12	33
44	10	12	20	20
+21	+ 9	+ 4	+33	+ 6

36	12	25	11	32
20	40	32	16	12
+13	+ 4	+ 1	+20	+22

25	10	44	30	21
11	24	11	24	37
+43	+ 5	+22	+14	+30

Lesson 3.5 Problem Solving

Solve each problem.

Lanie has 10 🦕.

Tina has 12 🦕. Paul has 25 🦕.

How many 🦕 do they have in all? __47__

$$\begin{array}{r} 10 \\ 12 \\ + 25 \\ \hline 47 \end{array}$$

The toy store sold 14 🤖 in March,

15 🤖 in April, and 20 🤖 in May.

How many 🤖 did the toy store sell in all? _____

Felicia puts 6 🪆, 22 🧸, and

30 🐘 on shelves. How many toys

does Felicia put on shelves? _____

The toy store has 32 🚗, 26 🚚,

and 10 🚜. How many of these toys

does the toy store have in all? _____

The bakery sells 14 🧁 on Monday, 23 🧁

on Tuesday, and 30 🧁 on Wednesday.

How many 🧁 did the bakery sell? _____

Add the ones.	Put the ones in the ones place. Put the tens in the tens place.		Add the tens.

Add the ones.		Put the ones in the ones place. Put the tens in the tens place.	Add the tens.
37 7 +45 +5 ? 12 12 = 1 ten 2 ones		1 37 +45 2	1 37 +45 sum → 82
46 6 +29 +9 ? 15 15 = 1 ten 5 ones		1 46 +29 5	1 46 +29 sum → 75

Add.

15 +66 81	48 +44	29 +35	19 +18	43 +39
75 +17	88 + 8	47 +37	26 +55	27 + 9
65 + 7	34 +28	46 + 5	69 +23	36 +49
54 +16	14 +59	45 +25	24 + 6	33 +58

NAME _____

Lesson 4.2 Problem Solving

Solve each problem.

Cara has 35 ✏.

Ben has 39 🖊.

How many 🖊 do they have in all? __74__

```
  1
  35
+ 39
-----
  74
```

Marcus has 48 📮.

May has 36 📮.

Together, they use 30 📮 to mail cards.

How many 📮 do they have left? _____

Pedro picks 33 🌼.

Jessica picks 28 🌼.

How many 🌼 do they pick in all? _____

There are 24 students with ⚽ or 🏈.   9 + _____ = 24

There are 9 students with 🏈.

How many students have ⚽? _____

Toya picks 15 🍎.

Jon picks 16 🍎.

How many 🍎 do they pick in all? _____

Lesson 4.3 Subtracting 2-Digit Numbers

		Rename 1 ten as 10 ones.	Subtract the ones.	Subtract the tens.
33 −19 3 tens 3 ones = 2 tens 13 ones		$\overset{2\ 13}{\cancel{33}}$ −19	$\overset{2\ 13}{\cancel{33}}$ −19 4	$\overset{2\ 13}{\cancel{33}}$ −19 difference → 14
60 −28 6 tens 0 ones = 5 tens 10 ones		$\overset{5\ 10}{\cancel{60}}$ −28	$\overset{5\ 10}{\cancel{60}}$ −28 2	$\overset{5\ 10}{\cancel{60}}$ −28 difference → 32

Subtract.

$\overset{2\ 16}{36}$
− 7
___
29

51	44	84	72
−39	−15	−47	−65

76	90	53	94	75
−19	−78	−26	−85	−18

44	83	64	50	97
−29	−46	−59	−29	−78

66	32	40	57	61
−28	−17	−25	−29	− 5

Lesson 4.4 Problem Solving

SHOW YOUR WORK

Solve each problem.

Freddie finds 33 🐌.

Tina finds 28 🐌.

How many more 🐌 does Freddie find? __5__

$$\begin{array}{r} 2\ 13 \\ \cancel{3}\cancel{3} \\ -\ 2\ 8 \\ \hline 5 \end{array}$$

Adam picks up 25 🐚 on Monday and 27 🐚 on Tuesday.

19 of the 🐚 are broken.

How many of the 🐚 are not broken? _____

Becky has 31 🥜.

She eats 8 🥜.

How many 🥜 does she have left? _____

William has 26 🚗.

He gave some 🚗 to a friend.

Now he has only 18 🚗.

How many 🚗 did William give to his friend? _____

$26 - $ _____ $= 18$

Connie counts 42 🐟.

Annie counts 27 🐟.

How many more 🐟 does Connie count? _____

Lesson 5.1 Counting and Writing 150 through 199

1 hundred + 5 tens + 3 ones = 153
Expanded Form: 100 + 50 + 3 = 153

Write the number and its expanded form.

  165

   _____

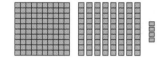 
100 + 60 + 5 = 165

___ + ___ + ___ = ___

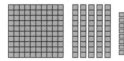 _____

___ + ___ + ___ = ___

___ + ___ + ___ = ___

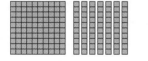 _____

 _____

___ + ___ + ___ = ___

___ + ___ + ___ = ___

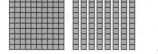 _____

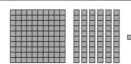 _____

___ + ___ + ___ = ___

___ + ___ + ___ = ___

Lesson 5.2 Counting and Writing 200 through 399

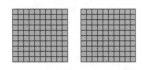

200
Number Name: two hundred

300
Number Name: three hundred

Write the number and the number name.

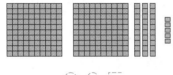

2 3 5
_____

two hundred thirty-five
_____

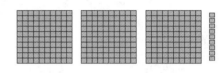

_____

_____

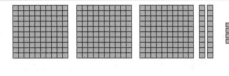

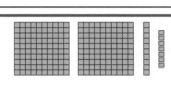

_____

_____

_____

_____

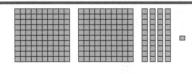

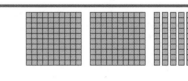

_____

_____

_____

_____

Lesson 5.3 Counting and Writing 400 through 699

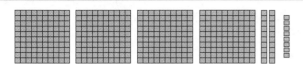

428

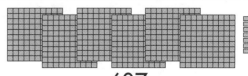

607

Number Name:
four hundred twenty-eight

Number Name:
six hundred seven

Write the number and the number name.

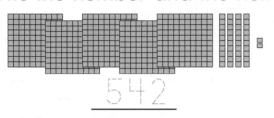

5 4 2
_____

five hundred forty-two
_____

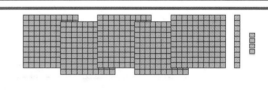

_____

_____

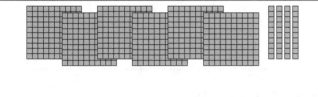

_____

_____

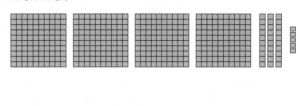

_____

_____

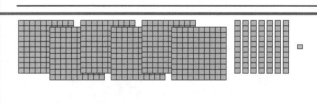

_____

_____

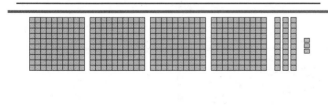

_____

_____

_____

_____

Lesson 5.4 Counting and Writing 700 through 999

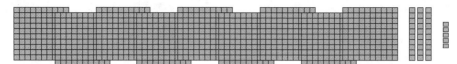

9 hundreds   3 tens   5 ones = 935
Expanded Form: 900 + 30 + 5 = 935

Write the number and its expanded form.

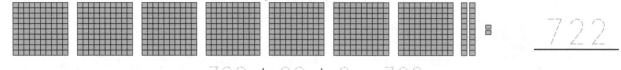   *722*

700 + *20* + *2* = *722*

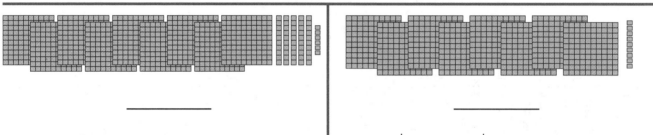

_____

____ + ____ + ____ = ____   ____ + ____ + ____ = ____

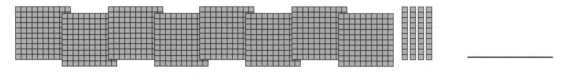

_____

____ + ____ + ____ = ____

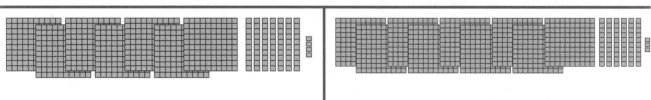

_____   _____

____ + ____ + ____ = ____   ____ + ____ + ____ = ____

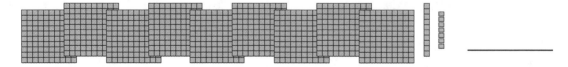

_____

____ + ____ + ____ = ____

Lesson 5.5 Skip Counting

Count 3-digit numbers by 1.

Start at 310.

310, 311, 312, 313, 314, _____, _____, 317

Start at 415.

415, 416, 417, 418, _____, 420, _____, 422

Skip count 3-digit numbers.

Count by 5. Start at 600.

600, 605, 610, _____, _____, 625, 630, _____

Count by 5. Start at 780.

780, 785, 790, _____, 800, 805, _____, _____

Count by 10. Start at 200.

200, 210, _____, 230, _____, 250, _____, 270

Count by 10. Start at 350.

350, 360, 370, _____, _____, 400, _____, _____

Count by 100. Start at 100.

100, 200, 300, _____, _____, 600, _____

Count backward by 100. Start at 900.

900, 800, 700, _____, 500, _____, _____

Lesson 5.5 Skip Counting

Skip count 3-digit numbers.

Count by 5. Start at 400.

400, 405, _____, _____, _____, 425, 430, _____, _____

Count by 10. Start at 310.

310, _____, _____, _____, 350, 360, _____

Count backward by 10. Start at 670.

670, _____, _____, _____, 630, 620, _____

Count backward by 10. Start at 532.

532, 522, 512, _____, _____, 482, _____, _____,

Count by 100. Start at 240.

240, 340, _____, _____, 640, _____, _____

Count by 100. Start at 110.

110, _____, _____, 410, _____, _____, _____

Count backward by 100. Start at 950.

950, _____, _____, _____, _____, 450, _____

Count backward by 100. Start at 826.

826, _____, _____, 526, _____, _____, 226

Lesson 5.6 Comparing Numbers

5̲03 [>] 3̲62   Compare hundreds. 5 is greater than 3. 503 is greater than 362.

73̲9 [<] 76̲1   If hundreds are the same, compare tens. 3 is less than 6. 739 is less than 761.

80̲1 [<] 80̲3   If hundreds and tens are the same, compare ones. 1 is less than 3. 801 is less than 803.

Compare 3-digit numbers. Use > (greater than), < (less than), or = (equal to).

831 [<] 843	436 [ ] 379	902 [ ] 911
567 [ ] 564	306 [ ] 401	535 [ ] 535
219 [ ] 198	739 [ ] 730	630 [ ] 820
127 [ ] 119	407 [ ] 610	923 [ ] 925
354 [ ] 453	802 [ ] 792	236 [ ] 401
504 [ ] 504	402 [ ] 408	123 [ ] 118
367 [ ] 562	760 [ ] 740	654 [ ] 736
981 [ ] 901	391 [ ] 491	835 [ ] 830

Lesson 5.7 Subtracting 2 Digits from 3 Digits

Subtract the ones.	To subtract the tens, rename the 1 hundred and 2 tens as 12 tens.	Subtract the tens.	

$$\begin{array}{r} 1\,2\,5 \\ -\quad 8\,4 \\ \hline \end{array}$$
$$\begin{array}{r} 1\,2\,5 \\ -\quad 8\,4 \\ \hline 1 \end{array}$$
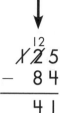
$$\begin{array}{r} {}^{12}\llap{\diagup}1\,2\,5 \\ -\quad 8\,4 \\ \hline 1 \end{array}$$
$$\begin{array}{r} {}^{12}\llap{\diagup}1\,2\,5 \\ -\quad 8\,4 \\ \hline 4\,1 \end{array}$$

minuend
subtrahend
difference

Subtract.

$$\begin{array}{r} 1\,7\,3 \\ -\quad 3\,3 \\ \hline 1\,4\,0 \end{array}$$
$$\begin{array}{r} 1\,2\,1 \\ -\quad 6\,0 \\ \hline \end{array}$$
$$\begin{array}{r} 1\,9\,5 \\ -\quad 4\,4 \\ \hline \end{array}$$
$$\begin{array}{r} 1\,2\,2 \\ -\quad 1\,1 \\ \hline \end{array}$$
$$\begin{array}{r} 1\,4\,7 \\ -\quad 5\,3 \\ \hline \end{array}$$

$$\begin{array}{r} 1\,4\,3 \\ -\quad 6\,2 \\ \hline \end{array}$$
$$\begin{array}{r} 1\,8\,0 \\ -\quad 7\,0 \\ \hline \end{array}$$
$$\begin{array}{r} 1\,1\,9 \\ -\quad 1\,5 \\ \hline \end{array}$$
$$\begin{array}{r} 1\,2\,3 \\ -\quad 1\,2 \\ \hline \end{array}$$
$$\begin{array}{r} 1\,8\,6 \\ -\quad 6\,5 \\ \hline \end{array}$$

$$\begin{array}{r} 1\,5\,4 \\ -\quad 1\,3 \\ \hline \end{array}$$
$$\begin{array}{r} 1\,2\,7 \\ -\quad 8\,3 \\ \hline \end{array}$$
$$\begin{array}{r} 1\,8\,7 \\ -\quad 6\,7 \\ \hline \end{array}$$
$$\begin{array}{r} 1\,3\,5 \\ -\quad 4\,2 \\ \hline \end{array}$$
$$\begin{array}{r} 1\,1\,5 \\ -\quad 2\,4 \\ \hline \end{array}$$

$$\begin{array}{r} 1\,3\,2 \\ -\quad 5\,1 \\ \hline \end{array}$$
$$\begin{array}{r} 1\,7\,7 \\ -\quad 4\,3 \\ \hline \end{array}$$
$$\begin{array}{r} 1\,9\,2 \\ -\quad 7\,1 \\ \hline \end{array}$$
$$\begin{array}{r} 1\,8\,6 \\ -\quad 9\,2 \\ \hline \end{array}$$
$$\begin{array}{r} 1\,3\,4 \\ -\quad 7\,2 \\ \hline \end{array}$$

$$\begin{array}{r} 1\,2\,9 \\ -\quad 8\,6 \\ \hline \end{array}$$
$$\begin{array}{r} 1\,7\,6 \\ -\quad 7\,5 \\ \hline \end{array}$$
$$\begin{array}{r} 1\,2\,0 \\ -\quad 4\,0 \\ \hline \end{array}$$
$$\begin{array}{r} 1\,9\,4 \\ -\quad 5\,3 \\ \hline \end{array}$$
$$\begin{array}{r} 1\,8\,9 \\ -\quad 6\,2 \\ \hline \end{array}$$

$$\begin{array}{r} 1\,6\,5 \\ -\quad 5\,1 \\ \hline \end{array}$$
$$\begin{array}{r} 1\,6\,7 \\ -\quad 4\,5 \\ \hline \end{array}$$
$$\begin{array}{r} 1\,5\,0 \\ -\quad 3\,0 \\ \hline \end{array}$$
$$\begin{array}{r} 1\,5\,7 \\ -\quad 6\,3 \\ \hline \end{array}$$
$$\begin{array}{r} 1\,4\,9 \\ -\quad 6\,1 \\ \hline \end{array}$$

Lesson 5.8 Adding 3-Digit Numbers

	Add the ones.	Add the tens.	Add the hundreds.
755 +469	7̇5̇5̇ +469 —— 4	7̇5̇5̇ +469 —— 24	7̇5̇5̇ + 469 —— 1224

Add.

123 +562 —— 685	982 +171	342 +591	782 +341	123 +321
862 +313	900 +130	720 +850	931 +111	823 +457
861 +421	862 +139	431 +250	782 +191	751 +605
791 +191	144 +800	192 +175	257 +147	203 +211
705 +719	641 +209	873 +505	700 +650	105 +341
593 +741	861 +209	735 +145	820 +431	738 +387

Lesson 5.9 Subtracting 3-Digit Numbers

Rename 2 tens and 1 one as 1 ten and 11 ones. Then, subtract the ones.

Rename 6 hundreds and 1 ten as 5 hundreds and 11 tens. Then, subtract the tens.

Subtract the hundreds.

```
    6 2 1          6̶ 2̶ 1̶          6̶ 2̶ 1̶          6̶ 2̶ 1̶   minuend
  − 2 5 9        − 2 5 9        − 2 5 9        − 2 5 9   subtrahend
                         2             6 2          3 6 2   difference
```

Subtract.

```
   3 2 1        7 4 5        6 3 9        8 3 0        6 2 6
 − 1 0 9      − 1 5 2      − 1 5 0      − 7 1 0      − 1 4 6
```

```
   7 2 9        6 5 7        3 8 6        4 1 1        4 8 6
 − 3 2 1      − 4 5 1      − 1 0 7      − 3 0 5      − 1 0 9
```

```
   9 8 3        9 7 1        8 7 6        5 4 9        7 2 1
 − 6 5 2      − 5 7 2      − 3 5 7      − 3 6 0      − 1 4 4
```

```
   2 5 6        3 4 7        7 2 5        8 6 3        9 8 0
 − 1 4 2      − 1 3 9      − 1 9 6      − 6 9 2      − 5 3 2
```

```
   5 4 3        7 6 2        1 3 2        9 2 1        6 3 1
 − 4 5 7      − 1 3 5      − 1 0 7      − 5 7 1      − 5 4 5
```

```
   5 3 1        7 2 0        5 8 2        7 9 3        6 1 2
 − 2 5 0      − 3 7 1      − 3 5 7      − 4 5 7      − 4 8 3
```

Lesson 5.10 Checking Addition with Subtraction

To check

215 + 109 = 324,

subtract 109 from 324.

```
   2 1 5
 + 1 0 9
 -------
   3 2 4      These should be the same.
 - 1 0 9
 -------
   2 1 5
```

Add. Check each answer.

```
   1 5 7        7 1 9        3 1 2        2 1 3        3 0 6
 + 2 1 2      + 1 8 2      + 1 0 5      + 5 1 9      + 2 1 5
 -------      -------      -------      -------      -------
   3 6 9
 - 2 1 2
 -------
   1 5 7
```

```
   7 1 0        3 5 7        7 1 2        7 1 4        3 1 2
 + 3 9 8      + 2 4 9      + 3 6 3      + 2 9 1      +   8 5
 -------      -------      -------      -------      -------
```

```
   3 0 0        5 9 1        6 1 2        4 2 5        4 1 1
 + 5 4 7      + 1 2 0      + 3 1 9      + 1 2 5      + 1 2 0
 -------      -------      -------      -------      -------
```

```
   8 6 3        4 5 9        6 0 3        7 1 1        2 5 2
 + 1 9 2      + 1 3 0      + 2 0 9      + 1 9 1      + 1 3 0
 -------      -------      -------      -------      -------
```

Lesson 5.11 Checking Subtraction with Addition

To check

982 − 657 = 325,

add 657 to 325.

$$
\begin{array}{r}
982 \\
-657 \\
\hline
325 \\
+657 \\
\hline
982
\end{array}
$$

These should be the same.

Subtract. Check each answer.

$$
\begin{array}{r}
720 \\
-150 \\
\hline
570 \\
+150 \\
\hline
720
\end{array}
$$

$$
\begin{array}{r}
321 \\
-\ 83 \\
\hline
\end{array}
$$

$$
\begin{array}{r}
125 \\
-\ 92 \\
\hline
\end{array}
$$

$$
\begin{array}{r}
983 \\
-657 \\
\hline
\end{array}
$$

$$
\begin{array}{r}
456 \\
-291 \\
\hline
\end{array}
$$

$$
\begin{array}{r}
300 \\
-179 \\
\hline
\end{array}
$$

$$
\begin{array}{r}
119 \\
-104 \\
\hline
\end{array}
$$

$$
\begin{array}{r}
423 \\
-197 \\
\hline
\end{array}
$$

$$
\begin{array}{r}
259 \\
-147 \\
\hline
\end{array}
$$

$$
\begin{array}{r}
592 \\
-463 \\
\hline
\end{array}
$$

$$
\begin{array}{r}
519 \\
-120 \\
\hline
\end{array}
$$

$$
\begin{array}{r}
540 \\
-320 \\
\hline
\end{array}
$$

$$
\begin{array}{r}
192 \\
-\ 86 \\
\hline
\end{array}
$$

$$
\begin{array}{r}
710 \\
-447 \\
\hline
\end{array}
$$

$$
\begin{array}{r}
683 \\
-419 \\
\hline
\end{array}
$$

$$
\begin{array}{r}
719 \\
-532 \\
\hline
\end{array}
$$

$$
\begin{array}{r}
919 \\
-457 \\
\hline
\end{array}
$$

$$
\begin{array}{r}
687 \\
-250 \\
\hline
\end{array}
$$

$$
\begin{array}{r}
912 \\
-609 \\
\hline
\end{array}
$$

$$
\begin{array}{r}
542 \\
-327 \\
\hline
\end{array}
$$

Chapter 6

Lesson 6.1 Telling Time to the Hour

   4 o'clock
4:00

Both clocks show 4 o'clock, or 4:00.

Write the time two ways.

_7_ o'clock 7:00	_____ o'clock _____ : _____	_____ o'clock _____ : _____

_____ o'clock _____ : _____	_____ o'clock _____ : _____	_____ o'clock _____ : _____

_____ o'clock _____ : _____	_____ o'clock _____ : _____	_____ o'clock _____ : _____

Lesson 6.2 Telling Time to the Half Hour

7 o'clock   half past 7   8 o'clock
7:00   7:30   8:00

Write the time two ways.

half past 4   half past_____   half past_____

 4:30   ____ : ____   ____ : ____

half past_____   half past_____   half past_____

____ : ____   ____ : ____   ____ : ____

half past_____   half past_____   half past_____

____ : ____   ____ : ____   ____ : ____

Lesson 6.3 Telling Time to the Quarter Hour

1:15
one fifteen

1:45
one forty-five

Read the time on the first clock.
Write the same time on the second clock.

6:45

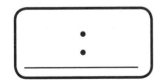

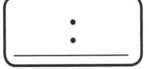

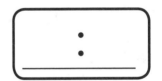

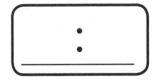

Lesson 6.3 Problem Solving

Solve each problem.

The small hand is between ___3___ and ___4___.

The large hand is on the ___6___.

The time is ___3:30___.

The small hand is between _____ and _____.

The large hand is on the _____.

The time is _____:_____.

The small hand is on the _____.

The large hand is on the _____.

The time is _____:_____.

The small hand is between _____ and _____.

The large hand is on the _____.

The time is _____:_____.

The small hand is on the _____.

The large hand is on the _____.

The time is _____:_____.

Lesson 6.4 Estimating Inches

Estimate how many inches long each object is.

 _____ inch

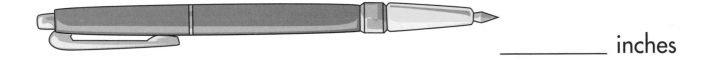 _____ inches

 _____ inches

 _____ inches

 _____ inches

_____ inches

Lesson 6.5 Estimating Centimeters

Estimate how many centimeters long each object is.

_____2_____ cm

_____ cm

_____ cm

_____ cm

_____ cm

_____ cm

Lesson 6.6 Measuring Length in Inches

Write the length of each object in inches.

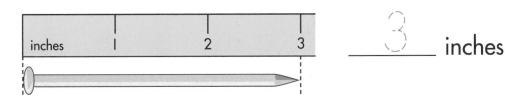

_____3_____ inches

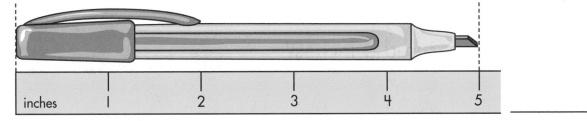

_____ inches

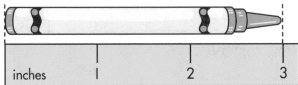

_____ inches

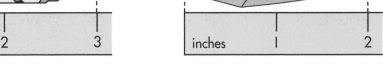

_____ inches

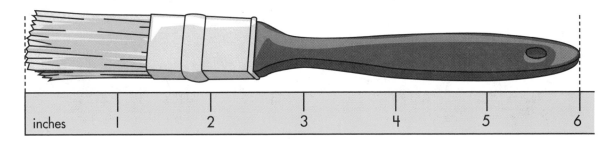

_____ inches

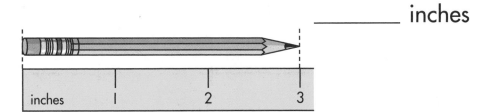

_____ inch

_____ inches

Lesson 6.7 Making a Line Plot

Answer the questions below using the previous page.

How many objects measured 1 inch? _____

How many objects measured 2 inches? _____

How many objects measured 3 inches? _____

How many objects measured 4 inches? _____

How many objects measured 5 inches? _____

How many objects measured 6 inches? _____

Make a line plot using the information above.

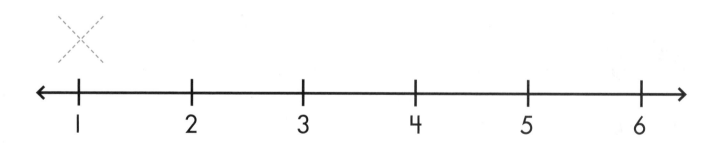

Lesson 6.8 Measuring Length in Inches

Perimeter is the length
around an object.
The perimeter of this hexagon is
1 + 1 + 1 + 1 + 1 + 1 = 6 inches.

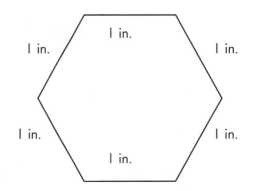

Use an inch ruler to measure length.

_____ inch

_____ inches

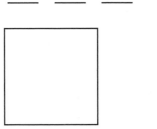

_____ inches

_____ inches

Measure the length of each side.
Add the lengths of all sides to get the perimeter.

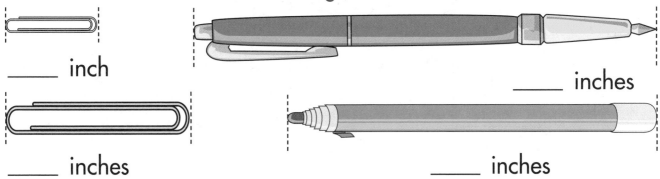

_3_ + _1_ + _3_ + _1_ = _8_ inches

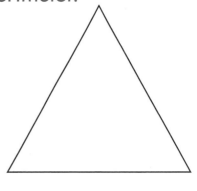

__ + __ + __ = __ inches

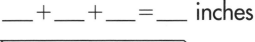

__ + __ + __ + __ = __ inches   __ + __ + __ + __ = __ inches

Lesson 6.9 Making a Line Plot

Create a line plot using the length of each shape.

4 in.

9 in.

3 in.

6 in.

4 in.

6 in.

3 in.

$$\longleftarrow \overset{|}{1} \quad \overset{|}{2} \quad \overset{|}{3} \quad \overset{|}{4} \quad \overset{|}{5} \quad \overset{|}{6} \quad \overset{|}{7} \quad \overset{|}{8} \quad \overset{|}{9} \longrightarrow$$

Lesson 6.10 Measuring Length in Centimeters

Write the length of each object in centimeters.

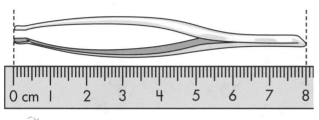

0 cm 1 2 3 4 5 6 7 8

__8__ centimeters

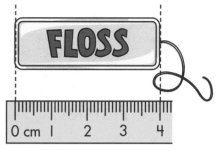

0 cm 1 2 3 4

____ centimeters

0 cm 1 2 3 4 5 6 7

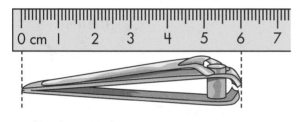

____ centimeters

0 cm 1 2 3 4 5 6 7 8 9

____ centimeters

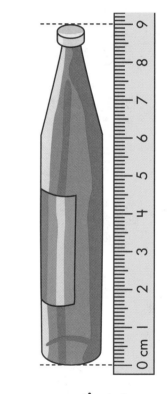

____ centimeters

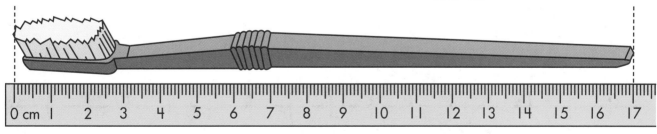

0 cm 1 2 3 4 5 6 7 8 9 10 11 12 13 14 15 16 17

____ centimeters

Lesson 6.11 Making a Line Plot

Create a line plot based on the measurements below.

__7__ centimeters

__5__ centimeters

__12__ centimeters

__8__ centimeters

__14__ centimeters

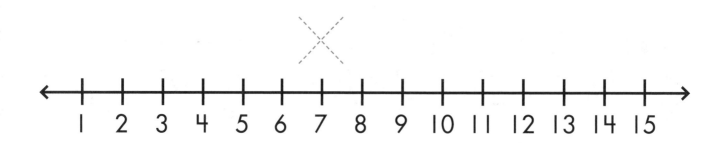

1 2 3 4 5 6 7 8 9 10 11 12 13 14 15

Lesson 6.12 Measuring Length in Centimeters

You can measure perimeter in centimeters.

The perimeter of this triangle is

3 + 3 + 3 = 9 centimeters.

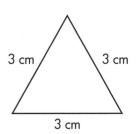
3 cm   3 cm
3 cm

Use a centimeter ruler to measure length.

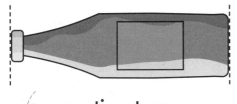

_6_ centimeters

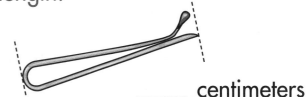

_____ centimeters

_____ centimeters

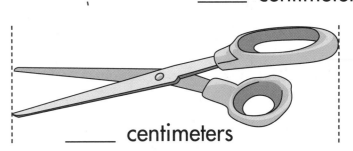

_____ centimeters

Measure perimeter. Add the lengths of all sides.

_6_ + _2_ + _6_ + _2_ = _16_ cm

___ + ___ + ___ + ___ = ___ cm

___ + ___ + ___ + ___ = ___ cm

___ + ___ + ___ + ___ + ___ = ___ cm

Lesson 6.13 Making a Line Plot

Create a line plot using the length of each shape.

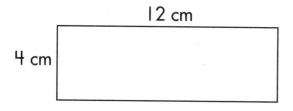

12 cm

4 cm

10 cm

2 cm

5 cm

5 cm

2 cm

7 cm

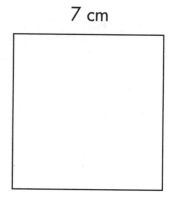

←——|——|——|——|——|——|——|——|——|——|——|——|——→
  1   2   3   4   5   6   7   8   9 10 11 12

Lesson 6.14 How Much Longer?

Measure each object. Tell how much longer one object is than the other.

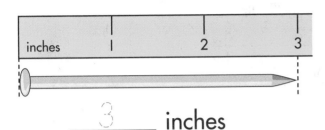

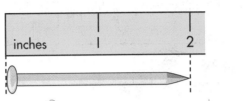

$$\begin{array}{r} 3 \\ -2 \\ \hline 1 \end{array}$$

___3___ inches ___2___ inches ___1___ inch longer

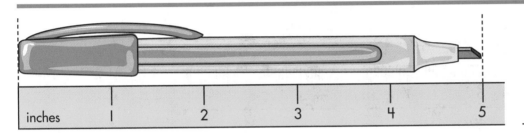

_____ inches

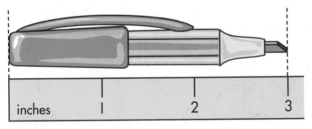

_____ inches

_____ inches longer

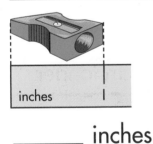

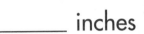

_____ inches

_____ inches longer

_____ inches

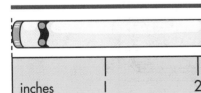

_____ inches

_____ inches longer

_____ inches

Lesson 6.14 How Much Longer?

Measure each object. Tell how much longer one object is than the other.

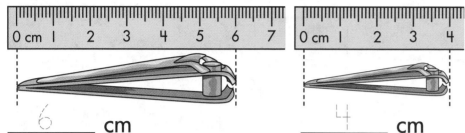

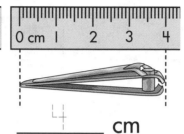

$$\begin{array}{r} 6 \\ -4 \\ \hline 2 \end{array}$$

_____6_____ cm   _____4_____ cm   __2__ cm longer

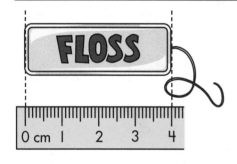

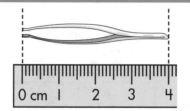

_____ cm   _____ cm   ___ cm longer

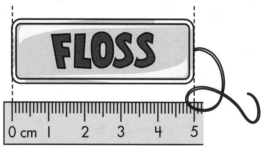

_____ cm   _____ cm   ___ cm longer

_____ cm   _____ cm   ___ cm longer

Lesson 6.15 Comparing Measurements

Use a ruler to measure each object in centimeters. Then, measure again using the line of squares.

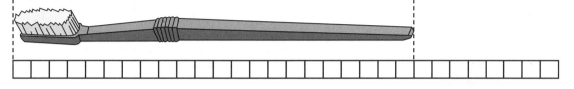

_____ centimeters   22 squares

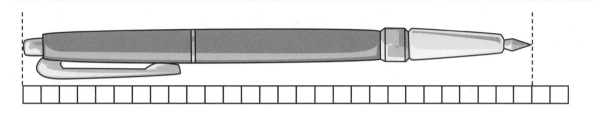

_____ centimeters   _____ squares

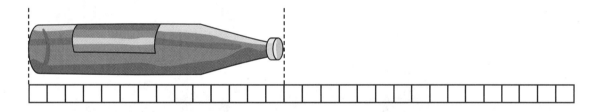

_____ centimeters   _____ squares

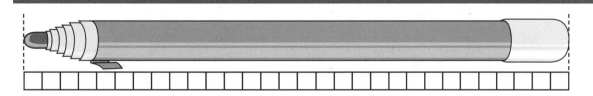

_____ centimeters   _____ squares

What do you notice about the measurements in centimeters compared to those in squares? _____

What explains this? _____

Lesson 6.15 Comparing Measurements

Use a ruler to measure each object in centimeters. Then, measure again to the nearest inch.

 _____ centimeters   about _____ inch

_____ centimeters   about _____ inches

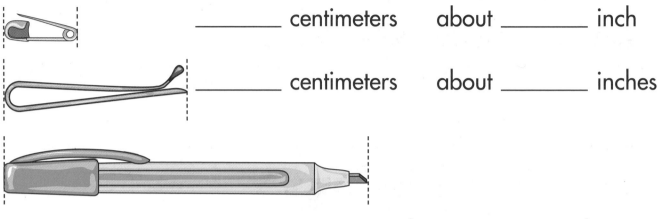

_____ centimeters   about _____ inches

_____ centimeters   about _____ inches

_____ centimeters   about _____ inches

_____ centimeters   about _____ inches

What do you notice about the measurements in centimeters compared to those in inches? _____

What explains this? _____

Lesson 6.16 Problem Solving

Solve each problem.

$$\begin{array}{r} 48 \\ +21 \\ \hline 69 \end{array}$$

Ryan has 48 feet of ribbon.

Sierra has 21 feet of ribbon.

How many feet of ribbon do they have altogether? __69__

Miranda has 11 inches of border for the bulletin board.

She needs 27 inches.

How much more border does
Miranda need to finish the bulletin board? _____

A fisherman had 20 feet of fishing line.

His line got stuck, and he had to cut away 13 feet.

How many feet of fishing line does the fisherman
have left? _____

Lindsey's necklace measured 17 inches.

Dominique's necklace measured 25 inches.

How much longer is Dominique's
necklace than Lindsey's? _____

Alfonzo's belt is 55 inches long.

Joshua's belt is 70 inches long.

How much longer is Joshua's belt than Alfonzo's? _____

Lesson 6.17 Reading Picture and Bar Graphs

Keisha asked her classmates about their pets.

She made this bar graph to show the results.

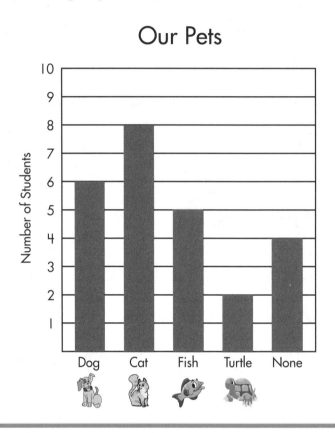

Our Pets

Use the bar graph to answer the questions.

How many students have a dog or a cat? ___14___

How many students have no pets? _____

Which pet do the most students have? _____

How many students have either a fish or turtle? _____

How many students did Keisha talk to? _____

Lesson 6.17 Reading Picture and Bar Graphs

Carlos polled his classmates about their favorite fruits.

He made this picture graph with the results. One piece of fruit

on the graph means one person.

Our Favorite Fruits

Apples	🍎 🍎 🍎 🍎
Oranges	🍊 🍊 🍊 🍊 🍊 🍊
Bananas	🍌 🍌 🍌 🍌
Grapes	🍇 🍇 🍇
Pears	🍐 🍐 🍐 🍐

Use the picture graph to answer the questions.

How many classmates chose either bananas or oranges? __10__

How many chose grapes or pears? _____

Which fruit did the most classmates choose? _____

How many classmates did not choose oranges? _____

How many more chose apples than chose grapes? _____

How many classmates told Carlos their favorite fruit? _____

Lesson 6.17 Reading Picture and Bar Graphs

Sam and his friends collect baseball cards. This picture graph shows how many cards they have.

Our Baseball Cards

Sam	🃏 🃏 🃏 🃏 🃏
Tara	🃏 🃏 🃏 🃏
Kono	🃏 🃏 🃏 🃏 🃏 🃏
Trina	🃏 🃏 🃏

🃏 = 2 baseball cards

Use the picture graph to answer the questions.

How many cards do the friends have in all? __40__

How many cards does Sam have? _____

Who has the fewest cards? _____

How many cards does Kono have? _____

How many cards do Tara and Trina have together? _____

How many more cards do
Tara and Trina have together compared to Sam? _____

Lesson 6.18 Creating a Bar Graph

Use the information in the tally chart to complete the bar graph.

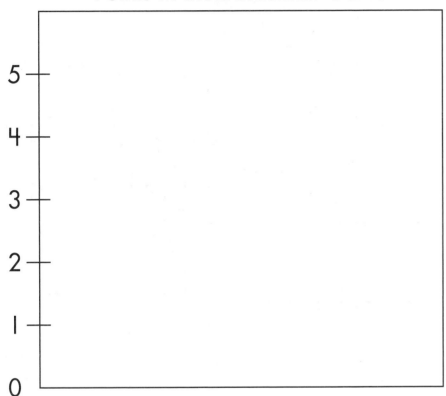

Points in the Basketball Game

Points in the Basketball Game	
Cara	III
Evan	++++
Dawn	IIII
Hugo	I

Use the bar graph to answer the questions.

Which student scored the most points? _____

Which student scored the least points? _____

How many points were scored
altogether in the basketball game? _____

How many more points did Evan score than Hugo? _____

Lesson 6.19 Creating a Picture Graph

Use the information in the tally chart to complete the picture graph.

Shapes Around the Room	
Triangles	
Stars	
Squares	
Circles	

Shapes Around the Room	
▲	⊬⊬ ∥
☆	⊬⊬ ⊬⊬
■	⊬⊬ ∥∥∥
●	⊬⊬ ∣

Use the picture graph to answer the questions below.

What shape is seen the most around the room? _____

What shape is seen the least around the room? _____

How many more stars ☆ are there than triangles ▲ ? _____

How many more squares ■ are there than circles ● ? _____

Lesson 6.20 Adding and Subtracting on a Number Line

Use the number line to add.

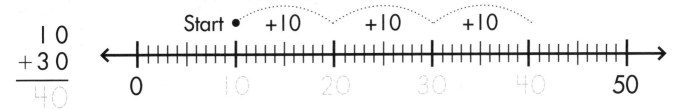

```
  1 0
+ 3 0
─────
  4 0
```

Use each number line to add or subtract.

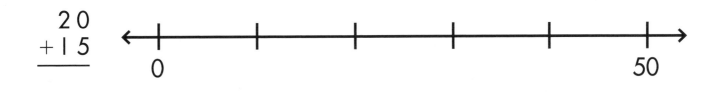

```
  5 0
- 2 0
─────
```

```
  2 0
+ 1 5
─────
```

```
  9 0
- 2 5
─────
```

```
  6 0
+ 1 3
─────
```

Chapter 7

Lesson 7.1 Plane Shapes

square	rectangle	triangle	circle

- 4 equal sides
- 4 right angles

- 2 pairs of equal sides
- 4 right angles

- 3 sides
- 3 angles

- no sides
- no angles

pentagon
- 5 sides
- 5 angles

hexagon
- 6 sides
- 6 angles

Name each shape.

<u>circle</u>   _____   _____   _____

_____   _____   _____   _____

Answer the questions.

Which shape has 4 equal sides? _____

Which shape has 6 angles? _____

Which shape has no angles? _____

Which shape has 3 sides? _____

NAME _____

Lesson 7.2 Solid Shapes

cube
- 6 square faces

rectangular
- 6 rectangular faces

square pyramid
- 4 triangular faces
- 1 square face

sphere
- no faces
- perfectly round

Circle the shape named.

rectangular solid

square pyramid

sphere

cube

Answer the questions about the shapes above.

Which shape has 4 triangular faces? _____

Which shape has 6 rectangular faces? _____

Which shape is like a 3-D circle? _____

Which shape has 6 equal faces? _____

Lesson 7.3 Drawing Plane Shapes

Draw plane shapes.

Look at the shape.	Draw your own shape. Color it.
 A triangle has 3 sides.	
 A square has 4 equal sides.	
 A rectangle has 2 pairs of equal sides.	
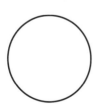 A circle is totally round.	

Lesson 7.4 Drawing Solid Shapes

Answer the questions.

What two plane shapes make up a square pyramid?

_____   _____

What plane shape is used to make a cube? _____

What two plane shapes can be part of a rectangular solid?

_____   _____

What plane shape is most like a sphere? _____

Look at the shape.	Draw your own shape. Color it.
 rectangular solid	
cube	
sphere	
square pyramid	

A shape can be broken into equal parts. These equal parts are called **fractions**.

A **half** is one of two equal parts. Two halves make a whole. ⊖.
The fraction **two-halves** means 2 out of 2 total parts, or $\frac{2}{2}$.

A **third** is one of three equal parts. Three thirds make a whole.

The fraction **three-thirds** means 3 out of 3 total parts, or $\frac{3}{3}$.

A **fourth** is one of four equal parts. Four fourths make a whole.

The fraction **four-fourths** means 4 out of 4 total parts, or $\frac{4}{4}$.

Write the fraction shown. Use numbers. Then, use words.

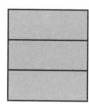

$\frac{3}{3}$, three-thirds _____

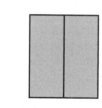

___ , _____

___ , _____

___ , _____

___ , _____

___ , _____

Lesson 8.2 One-Half

One-half of the whole
is shaded.

$\frac{1}{2}$ = **1** out of **2** equal parts

One-half of the whole
is shaded.

$\frac{1}{2}$ = **1** out of **2** equal parts

Complete.

There are ___2___ equal parts.

___1___ of the parts is shaded.

__1/2__ of the whole is shaded.

There are ___2___ equal parts.

___1___ of the parts is shaded.

__1/2__ of the whole is shaded.

There are _____ equal parts.

_____ of the parts is shaded.

___ _____ of the whole is shaded.

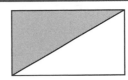

There are _____ equal parts.

_____ of the parts is shaded.

___ _____ of the whole is shaded.

Write the fraction that is shaded in words.

___One-half___ is shaded.

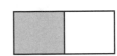

_____ is shaded.

Lesson 8.3 One-Third

One-third of the whole is shaded.

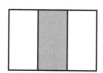

$\frac{1}{3} = $ **1** out of **3** equal parts

One-third of the whole is shaded.

$\frac{1}{3} = $ **1** out of **3** equal parts

Complete.

There are ___3___ equal parts.

___1___ of the parts is shaded.

___1___ of the whole is shaded.
$\frac{}{3}$

There are ___3___ equal parts.

___1___ of the parts is shaded.

___1___ of the whole is shaded.
$\frac{}{3}$

There are _____ equal parts.

_____ of the parts is shaded.

_____ of the whole is shaded.

There are _____ equal parts.

_____ of the parts is shaded.

_____ of the whole is shaded.

Write the fraction that is shaded in words.

____One-third____ is shaded.

_____ is shaded.

Lesson 8.4 One-Fourth

One-fourth of the whole is shaded.

$\frac{1}{4}$ = **1** out of **4** equal parts

One-fourth of the whole is shaded.

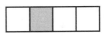

$\frac{1}{4}$ = **1** out of **4** equal parts

Complete.

There are ___4___ equal parts.

___1___ of the parts is shaded.

$\frac{1}{4}$ of the whole is shaded.

There are _____ equal parts.

_____ of the parts is shaded.

___ of the whole is shaded.

There are _____ equal parts.

_____ of the parts is shaded.

___ of the whole is shaded.

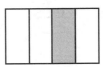

There are _____ equal parts.

_____ of the parts is shaded.

___ of the whole is shaded.

Write the fraction that is shaded in words.

One-fourth _____ is shaded.

_____ is shaded.

Lesson 8.5 Partitioning Rectangles

Rectangles can be divided up into same-size squares to show how much space they cover.

This rectangle is made up of 6 squares. It takes up 6 squares of space.

Count the squares ☐ that make up each rectangle.

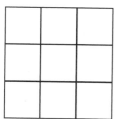  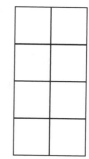

_9_ equal squares   _____ equal squares   _____ equal squares

---

Draw same-size squares ☐ to fill each rectangle. Then, count the number of squares.

_____ square units   _____ square units   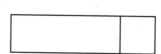_____ square units

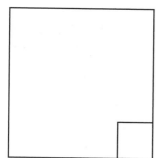   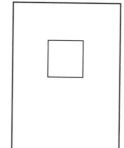   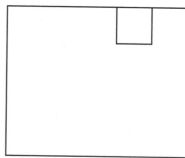

_____ square units   _____ square units   _____ square units

SPECTRUM®

Language Arts

Lesson 1.1 Common and Collective Nouns

A **noun** is a word that names a person, a place, or a thing.

> brother (person)   park (place)   bicycle (thing)

The nouns in the following sentences are in bold.

> The **teacher** gave us **work** to do.

> The **library** is next to the **pool**.

A **collective noun** is a word for a group of animals, things, or people.

> a **herd** of horses   a **deck** of cards   a **troupe** of actors

Identify It

Read the paragraph below. Circle each noun. There are 20 nouns.

I packed my bag for camp. I packed shirts, shorts, socks, and shoes. I added my toothbrush and a comb. My mom said to bring a hat. My dad said to bring a game and a book. I wanted to bring my cat. My mom and dad said cats do not go to camp. I brought a photo of my cat, instead.

Lesson 1.1 Common and Collective Nouns

Complete It

A collective noun is missing from each sentence below. Fill in each blank with a noun from the box.

fleet	**litter**	**school**
flock	**team**	**pod**

1. A _____ of birds landed in the apple tree.

2. Grace's cat gave birth to a _____ of six kittens.

3. A _____ of ships left the harbor at noon.

4. The _____ of hockey players boarded the bus.

5. The shark spotted a _____ of fish.

6. A _____ of dolphins leaped around the boat.

Try It

Write two sentences about what you would pack if you were going on a trip. Each sentence should have two nouns. Circle each noun.

1. _____

_____

2. _____

_____

Lesson 1.2 Proper Nouns

A **proper noun** is a noun that names a special person, place, or thing. Proper nouns begin with a capital letter to show that they are important. Here are some common and proper nouns.

Common Nouns	Proper Nouns
school	Thomas Jefferson Elementary School
sister	Emily
city	Capital City
dog	Bailey

Identify It

Read each sentence below. Underline the nouns. Write the letter **C** above each common noun. Write the letter **P** above each proper noun.

1. The students in my class are going on a trip.

2. We are going to the New England Museum.

3. I am going to sit near Carson, Maddy, and Maria on the bus.

4. Mr. Cohen said that we will have lunch in the cafeteria.

5. My family and I visited a museum when we went to Chicago.

Lesson 1.2 Proper Nouns

Proof It

Read the paragraph below. Remember, proper nouns begin with a capital letter. If they do not, underline the first letter three times. Then, write the capital letter above it.

Example: Max and e̲nrique went to b̲uxton Public Library after school.
(E above enrique, B above buxton)

Chicago is the largest city in illinois. It is near the shores of lake michigan. Aunt suzanne lives there. My sister, ellie, loves to visit her in chicago. They like to go to the museums. Uncle alex said I can come visit next time.

Try It

1. Write a sentence that tells about a place you have visited. Your sentence should contain one proper noun. Circle the proper noun.

_____

2. Now, write a sentence that tells about a place you would like to visit one day. It should also tell who you would like to bring along. Your sentence should contain two proper nouns. Circle the proper nouns.

_____

_____

Lesson 1.3 Pronouns

A **pronoun** is a word that takes the place of a noun. Some pronouns are **I, me, you, he, she, him, her, it, we, us, they,** and **them**.

In the sentences below, pronouns take the place of the underlined nouns.

<u>Drew and Lei</u> play softball every Saturday.
They play softball every Saturday.

Dad parked the <u>car</u> in the garage.
Dad parked **it** in the garage.

Reflexive pronouns end in **self** or **selves**.
Myself, yourself, himself, herself, itself, ourselves, and **themselves** are reflexive pronouns.

Identify It

Circle the pronouns in the following paragraph. There are 12 pronouns.

I will never forget the first soccer game I ever saw. Mom, Dad, Laura, and I drove downtown to the stadium. It was lit up against the night sky. We were excited to see the Rangers play. The stadium was filled with hundreds of people. They cheered when the players ran onto the field. Laura and I screamed and clapped ourselves silly. We laughed when the Rangers' mascot did a funny dance. The best part of the game was when Matt Ramos scored the winning goal. He is the best player on the team. It was a night to remember for myself and my family!

Lesson 1.3 Pronouns

Complete It

Read each pair of sentences below. Choose the correct pronoun from the pair in parentheses ( ) to take the place of the underlined word or words. Write it in the space.

1. Mom drove <u>Anna</u> to soccer practice. Mom drove _____ (you, her) to soccer practice.

2. <u>Dan and Marco</u> are on Anna's team. _____ (Him, They) are on Anna's team.

3. <u>Anna</u> kicked the ball out of bounds. _____ (She, Her) kicked the ball out of bounds.

4. The coach talked to <u>the players</u>. The coach talked to _____ (she, them).

Rewrite It

Fill in each blank below with a reflexive pronoun.

1. The team served _____ a snack after the game.

2. Anna cut _____ when she tripped over a rock.

3. Tim blamed _____ for not checking the field better.

4. "You should be proud of _____ for a great game!" said Coach.

Lesson 1.4 Verbs

Verbs are an important part of speech. They are often action words. They tell what happens in a sentence. The verbs in the sentences below are in bold.

Sadie **raced** down the stairs. She **barked** at the cat on the windowsill. Then, she **wagged** her tail at Mrs. Callahan. Sadie **ate** the treat from Mrs. Callahan's hand.

Solve It

Find the verb in each sentence. Write it in the spaces under the sentence.

1. Akiko placed her new puppy on the rug in the living room.

   _ _◯_ _ _

2. The puppy sniffed the rug and the couch.

   _◯_ _ _ _ _

3. The puppy ran in circles around the room.

   _ _◯

4. Akiko and her dad giggled at the excited little dog.

   _◯_ _ _ _ _

5. The puppy chewed on Akiko's green slipper.

   _ _ _ _◯_

What is Akiko's puppy's name? Write the circled letters from your answers on the lines below to spell out the puppy's name.

   _ _ _ _ _

Lesson 1.4 Verbs

Complete It

Fill in each blank with a verb from the box. Some
verbs can be used in more than one sentence.

ran	gave	played
took	threw	chased

1. Sam and Hailey _____ their dogs, Muffy and Baxter,
   to the park.

2. The dogs _____ in a pond.

3. They _____ around the park again and again.

4. Hailey _____ a stick.

5. Muffy and Baxter _____ the stick.

6. Sam and Hailey _____ Muffy and Baxter two big
   bones.

Try It

1. What else could Muffy and Baxter do at the park? Write another
   sentence. Circle the verb.

   _____

2. What do you think Sam and Hailey will do when they get home
   from the park? Write a sentence. Circle the verb.

   _____

Lesson 1.5 Adjectives

Adjectives are words that describe. They give more information about nouns. Adjectives often answer the question **What kind?**

Kyle has a shirt.   Kyle has a **striped** shirt.

The adjective **striped** tells **what kind** of shirt Kyle has.

The adjectives in the sentences below are in bold.

Linh put the **yellow** flowers on the **wooden** table.
Jess has **curly**, **red** hair.
The **bright** moon shone in the **dark** sky.

Match It

Choose the adjective from the second column that best describes each noun in the first column. Write the letter of the adjective on the line. Some answers can be used twice.

1. the _____ sunshine   a. green

2. the _____ bird   b. rough

3. the _____ grass   c. chirping

4. the _____ squirrel   d. warm

5. the _____ bark of the tree e. noisy

6. the _____ lawnmower   f. furry

> **Tip** Adjectives do not always come before nouns: **The sky is blue.** The adjective **blue** describes the noun **sky**, but it does not come right before it in the sentence.

Lesson 1.5 Adjectives

Identify It

Read the sentences below. Circle the adjectives. Then, underline the nouns the adjectives describe.

Example: Kirsten made some (cold,) (sweet) <u>lemonade</u>.

1. A large raccoon lives in the woods near my house.

2. Raccoons have four legs and bushy tails.

3. They have black patches on their faces.

4. It looks like they are wearing funny masks.

5. Raccoons also have dark rings on their tails.

6. They sleep in warm dens in the winter.

7. Raccoons eat fresh fruit, eggs, and insects.

Try It

1. Write a sentence that describes an animal you have seen in the wild. Use two adjectives.

   _____

   _____

2. Where do you think this animal lives? Write a sentence that describes the animal's home. Use two adjectives.

   _____

   _____

Lesson 1.6 Adverbs

Adverbs are words that describe verbs. Adverbs often answer the questions **When?**, **Where?**, or **How?**

> She **quickly** opened the umbrella.
> **Quickly** tells **how** the umbrella was opened.

> We will go to the museum **later**.
> **Later** tells **when** we will go to the museum.

> Maya ran **down** the street.
> **Down** tells **where** Maya ran.

Identify It

Circle the adverb in each sentence below. Then, decide if the adverb tells **when**, **where**, or **how**. Write **when**, **where**, or **how** on the line beside the sentence.

1. Yesterday, it snowed. _____

2. Big flakes fell gently to the ground. _____

3. Ian looked everywhere for his mittens. _____

4. He quickly put on his boots and hat. _____

5. He opened the door and walked outside. _____

6. Ian quietly listened to the snow falling. _____

| Tip | Adverbs often end with the letters **ly**. Here are some adverbs: **lightly**, **slowly**, **softly**, **evenly**, **joyfully**, and **loosely**. |

Lesson 1.6 Adverbs

Complete It

An adverb is missing from each sentence below. Choose the correct adverb from the words in parentheses ( ). Write it in the blank.

1. Ian _____ ran to his friend Ming's house. (quickly, quick)

2. He knocked _____ at the back door. (loud, loudly)

3. _____, Ming was ready to play in the snow. (Soon, Sooner)

4. Ming's brother, Jin, came home _____. (early, earliest)

5. He _____ joined Ming and Ian in the yard. (happy, happily)

6. _____, they built a snowman. (First, Last)

7. Jin _____ tossed a snowball at his sister. (playful, playfully)

8. Ming, Jin, and Ian went _____ for some hot cocoa. (inside, into)

Try It

Write a sentence that tells about something you did with your friends. Use at least one of these adverbs in your sentence: **slowly**, **quickly**, **loudly**, **quietly**, **easily**, **suddenly**, **before**, **later**, **after**, **sometimes**.

_____

Tip	When you are looking for the adverb in a sentence, sometimes it helps to find the verb first. Then, ask yourself **When?**, **Where?**, or **How?** about the verb.

Lesson 1.7 Statements

A **statement** is a sentence that begins with a capital letter and ends with a period. A statement tells the reader something. Each of the following sentences is a statement.

My brother and I fly kites when we go to the beach.
My kite is shaped like a diamond.
It is purple, blue, and green.
It has a long tail.

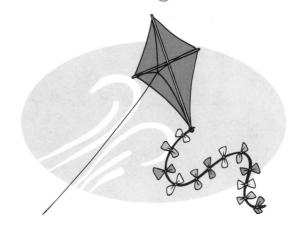

Rewrite It

Rewrite the following sentences. Each statement should begin with a capital letter and end with a period.

1. people have flown kites for thousands of years

   _____

   _____

2. some kites are shaped like dragons or fish

   _____

   _____

3. others are shaped like birds

   _____

4. flying kites is a fun hobby

   _____

Lesson 1.7 Statements

Proof It

Read the following paragraphs. Each statement should begin with a capital letter and end with a period. Use this proofreading mark (≡) under a letter to make it a capital. Use this proofreading mark (⊙) to add a period.

Example: nick and Matt made a kite shaped like a frog .
    N
    ≡

early kites were made in China. They were covered with silk Other kites were covered with paper. the material covering the wooden sticks was sometimes painted by hand

benjamin Franklin did experiments with kites Alexander Graham Bell also used kites in his experiments.

today, kite festivals are held in many cities. people come from all around the world They like to share their kites with other kite lovers. some kites are tiny Others measure as much as one hundred feet

Try It

1. What kind of kite would you make? Write a statement about it.

    _____

2. Where would you fly the kite? Write a statement about it.

    _____

Lesson 1.8 Questions

Questions are sentences that ask something. A question begins with a capital letter and ends with a question mark.

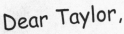

(W)here are your shoes(?)

(H)ave you seen my hat(?)

(D)id you put my mittens away(?)

Proof It

Read the letter below. Find the four periods that should be question marks. Write question marks in their place.

> Dear Taylor,
>
> How are you. I am having a great time on vacation. Have you ever been to Florida. I have never seen so many palm trees. Yesterday, we went to the ocean. Can you guess what I found on the beach. I found a jellyfish and sand dollar.
>
> We had a cookout with my cousins on Tuesday. I tried three kinds of fresh fish. Do you like fish. I like it more than I thought I would.
>
> That is all the news from Florida. I hope you are having a good vacation, too.
>
> Your friend,
>
> Isabel

Tip	Questions often begin with words like these: **who, what, when, where, why, how, did, do, will,** and **can**.

Lesson 1.8 Questions

Complete It

Read the sentences that follow. If a sentence is a statement, add a period on the line. If a sentence is a question, add a question mark on the line.

1. Isabel and her family drove to Florida___

2. Do you know how long it took them to get there___

3. They drove for three days___

4. Isabel has two sisters___

5. What did the girls do during the long drive___

6. Did they play games in the car___

7. Everyone in Isabel's family likes to sing___

8. Where will they go on vacation next year___

Try It

On the lines below, write two questions you could ask Isabel about her vacation. Make sure each question begins with a capital letter and ends with a question mark.

_____

_____

_____

_____

Lesson 1.9 Exclamations

Exclamations are sentences that are said with great feeling. They show excitement or surprise. Exclamations begin with a capital letter and end with an exclamation point.

Ⓡanisha won the race**!**

Ⓢ love your new jacket**!**

Ⓟhere is something scary under the bed**!**

Rewrite It

Rewrite the following sentences. Each exclamation should begin with a capital letter and end with an exclamation point.

1. we won the game

   _____

2. maggie hit six homeruns

   _____

3. she set a record

   _____

4. we are the school champions

   _____

Tip	Some exclamations can be a single word. **Surprise! Hurray! Ouch! No!**

Lesson 1.9 Exclamations

Proof It

Read the following diary entry. Find the six periods that should be exclamation points. Write exclamation points in their place.

Tuesday, April 7

Dear Diary,

Today began like any other day. I had no idea what was in store for me. I brought the mail in the house. There was a blue envelope. Hurray. It was just what I had been waiting for. I opened it and pulled out the letter. Here is what it said: Congratulations. You are the grand-prize winner.

I ran upstairs to find my mom. I could not wait to tell her the news. We had won a free vacation. I knew she would be amazed. I enter many contests. I do not usually win, though. What a great day.

Try It

Imagine that you are telling a friend about something exciting that happened to you. Write two sentences that are exclamations. Remember to begin with a capital letter and end with an exclamation point.

1. _____

_____

2. _____

_____

Lesson 1.10 Commands

Commands are sentences that tell you to do something. Commands begin with a capital letter. They end with a period.

Do not forget your lunch. **R**ead the other book first.

Close the door. **L**ook inside the box.

Statements usually begin with a noun or a pronoun. Commands often begin with a verb. Look at the examples above. The words **do**, **read**, **close**, and **look** are all verbs.

Identify It

Read each sentence below. If it is a command, write **C** on the line. If it is a statement, write **S** on the line.

1. Tia and her grandpa like to bake together. _____

2. They follow special rules in the kitchen. _____

3. Wash your hands after you touch raw eggs. _____

4. Be careful when the stove is hot. _____

5. Read the recipe before you begin. _____

6. Measure the ingredients. _____

7. Tia makes tasty oatmeal cookies. _____

8. Grandpa likes to make cornbread. _____

Lesson 1.10 Commands

Complete It

Each of the following commands is missing a word and an end mark. Choose the word from the box that best completes each command. Then, add the correct end mark.

Drink	Chop	Put
Fill	Blend	Turn

How to Make a Berry Good Smoothie

1. _____ a banana into small pieces__

2. _____ some berries and the banana pieces in the blender__

3. _____ the blender halfway with milk and orange juice__

4. _____ on the blender__

5. _____ the ingredients until they are smooth__

6. _____ the smoothie from a tall glass__

Try It

Think of two rules you need to follow at school. Write them as commands.

Example: Listen quietly when the teacher talks.

1. _____

2. _____

Lesson 1.11 Combining Sentences (Nouns)

Sometimes, sentences can be combined.

Bats eat bugs.   Frogs eat bugs.

Both sentences tell about things that eat insects. These two sentences can be combined into one by using the word **and**.

Bats **and** frogs eat bugs.

Here is another example.

Children like to go to the beach.
Adults like to go to the beach.
Children **and** adults like to go to the beach.

Identify It

Read each pair of sentences below. If the sentences can be joined with the word **and**, make a check mark (✓) on the line. If not, leave the line blank.

1. Blue jays visit my birdfeeder. Robins visit my birdfeeder. _____

2. Parrots live in warm places. Penguins live in cold places. _____

3. Hawks build nests on ledges. Eagles build nests on ledges. _____

4. Hummingbirds like flowers. Bees like flowers. _____

5. Geese fly south for the winter. Owls do not fly south in the winter. _____

Lesson 1.11 Combining Sentences (Nouns)

Rewrite It

Combine each pair of sentences below into one sentence. Write the new sentence.

1. Herons live near water. Mallards live near water.

   _____

2. Sparrows are mostly brown. Wrens are mostly brown.

   _____

3. Cardinals eat seeds. Finches eat seeds.

   _____

4. Crows are completely black. Grackles are completely black.

   _____

Try It

1. Think of two things that are the same in some way. They might be the same color or the same size. They might eat the same thing or like doing the same thing. Write a pair of sentences about the two things you chose.

   Example: Cats like to be petted.   Dogs like to be petted.

   _____   _____

2. Now, combine the two sentences you wrote into one.

   _____

Lesson 1.12 Combining Sentences (Verbs)

Sometimes sentences can be combined.

Julia bikes on Saturday morning.

Julia jogs on Saturday morning.

Both sentences tell what Julia does on Saturday morning. These two sentences can be joined using the word **and**.

Julia bikes **and** jogs on Saturday morning.

Complete It

Read the sentences below. Fill in each space with the missing word or words.

1. Mom carried out the birthday cake. Mom placed it on the table.

   _____ carried out the birthday cake _____

   placed it on the table.

2. Carmen took a deep breath. Carmen blew out the candles.

   _____ took a deep breath _____ blew out the

   candles.

3. The children sang "Happy Birthday." The children clapped for Carmen.

   _____ sang "Happy Birthday" _____

   clapped for Carmen.

Lesson 1.12 Combining Sentences (Verbs)

Rewrite It

Combine each pair of sentences below
into one sentence.

1. Carmen unwrapped her presents. Carmen opened the boxes.

   _____

2. Carmen smiled. Carmen thanked her friends for the gifts.

   _____

3. Everyone played freeze tag. Everyone had a good time.

   _____

4. The guests ate some cake. The guests drank pink lemonade.

   _____

Try It

1. Write two sentences that tell about things you do. Use a different
   verb in each sentence.

   Example: Carmen sings in a choir. Carmen plays the piano.

   _____   _____

2. Now, combine the two sentences you wrote using the word
   and.

   Example: Carmen sings in a choir and plays the piano.

   _____

Lesson 1.13 Combining Sentences (Adjectives)

Sometimes sentences can be combined.

The wagon was red.   The wagon was shiny.

The adjectives **red** and **shiny** both describe **wagon**. These two sentences can be combined into one by using the word **and**.

The wagon was red **and** shiny.

Here is another example.

Danny has a new scooter.   The scooter is blue.

The adjectives **new** and **blue** describe Danny's scooter. The two sentences can be combined.

Danny has a **new blue** scooter.

Identify It

Read each pair of sentences below. If the adjectives in both sentences describe the same person or thing, the sentences can be combined. Make a check mark (✓) on the line if the two sentences can be combined.

1. Oliver's painting is bright. Oliver's painting is cheerful. _____

2. Oliver painted the flower garden. The garden was colorful. _____

3. Oliver's paintbrush is soft. Oliver's paints are new. _____

4. The wall is large. The wall is white. _____

5. The tulips are red. The rosebushes are big. _____

Lesson 1.13 Combining Sentences (Adjectives)

Rewrite It

Combine each pair of sentences below into one sentence.

1. The paints are shiny. The paints are wet.

   _____

2. The afternoon is warm. The afternoon is sunny.

   _____

3. Oliver's paintings are beautiful. Oliver's paintings are popular.

   _____

4. The red tulips are Oliver's favorite. The tulips are pretty.

   _____

Try It

1. Write two sentences that describe your hair. Use a different adjective in each sentence.

   Example: My hair is red.   My hair is curly.

   _____   _____

2. Now write a sentence that combines the two sentences you wrote.

   Example: My hair is red and curly.

   _____

All sentences begin with a capital letter. A capital letter is a sign to the reader that a new sentence is starting.

(M)arisol colored the leaves with a green crayon.
(A)lexander loves to dance.

(T)he bus will arrive at three o'clock.
(I)s the book on the coffee table?

(I) love your backpack!
(R)aise your left hand.

Proof It

Read the paragraphs below. The first word of every sentence should begin with a capital letter. To show that a letter should be a capital, underline it three times (≡). Then, write the capital letter above it.

Example: your socks don't match.

tree trunks can tell the story of a tree's life. a slice of a tree trunk shows many rings. a tree adds a new ring every year. each ring has a light part and a dark part. when scientists look at the rings, they learn about the tree.

the rings can tell how old a tree is. they can tell what the weather was like. if there was a fire or a flood, the rings will show it. trees cannot talk, but they do tell stories.

Lesson 2.1 Capitalizing the First Word in a Sentence

Rewrite It

Rewrite each sentence below. Make sure your sentences begin with a capital letter.

1. the oldest living tree is in California.

   _____

2. it is located in the White Mountains.

   _____

3. the tree is more than 4,600 years old.

   _____

4. scientists named the tree Methuselah.

   _____

5. would you like to visit this tree one day?

   _____

Try It

1. Write a sentence about something very old. Be sure to start your sentence with a capital letter.

   _____

2. Write a sentence that explains one reason you like trees. Be sure to start your sentence with a capital letter.

   _____

Lesson 2.2 Capitalizing Names

The **name of a person or a pet** always begins with a capital letter.

(J)asper is (E)mily's brother.

The baby polar bear's name is (A)rthur.

Mom always buys (S)niffy's tissues.

Complete It

Complete each sentence below. Write each name in parentheses ( ). Remember to capitalize the names of people, pets, and products.

1. _____ (cassie's) favorite food is corn on the cob.

2. _____ (omar) loves olives and oranges.

3. _____ (peter's) pet parakeet, _____ (prudence), eats _____ (pet food plus) peanuts.

4. _____ (auntie ann's apple crunch) is _____ (amy's) favorite cereal.

5. _____ (bradley's) bunny, _____ (boris), eats beets.

6. _____ (tess) and _____ (tom) like _____ (tito's tasty tacos).

Lesson 2.2 Capitalizing Names

Proof It

Read the paragraph below. The names of people, pets, and products should begin with a capital letter. To show that a letter should be capital, underline it three times (≡). Then, write the capital letter above it.

The neighborhood was getting ready to have a pet show. Geoffrey and gina brushed their pet gerbil, george, with a groom-easy brush they bought at the pet store. hank and harry's hamster, hilda, was ready to perform all her tricks. Sandeep tightly held his snake, simon. The show was ready to start. Only frances and her flamingo, Flora, were still missing. frances had to finish giving flora a bath with clean critters shampoo. Finally, they arrived. The pet show could begin!

Try It

1. Write a sentence using the names of three of your friends.

   _____

2. Imagine you had one of the following pets: a hippo, a lion, a whale, a bear, or an anteater. Write a sentence about what you would name your pet.

   _____

Lesson 2.3 Capitalizing Titles

A **title** is a word that comes before a person's name. A title gives more information about who a person is. Titles that come before a name begin with a capital letter.

Grandma Sheryl   Uncle David

Cousin Ella   President George Washington

Doctor Wright   Judge Thomas

Titles of respect also begin with a capital letter. Here are some titles of respect: **Mr., Mrs., Ms.,** and **Miss.**

Mr. Garza   Miss Sullivan   Ms. Romano   Mrs. Chun

Proof It

Read the diary entry below. All titles should begin with a capital letter. To show that a letter should be a capital, underline it three times (≡). Then, write the capital letter above it.

Dear Diary,

Last night, I went to a play with aunt Sonia and uncle Pat. I sat next to cousin Fiona and cousin Nora. The play was about ms. Amelia Earhart, the first woman to fly across the Atlantic Ocean alone. ms. Earhart led an exciting life. She even met president Roosevelt.

After the play, I met Aunt Sonia's friend, mrs. Angley. She played the role of ms. Earhart. I also met mr. Roche. He played the role of president Roosevelt. He was very kind and funny.

Lesson 2.3 Capitalizing Titles

Rewrite It

Rewrite each of the following sentences.
Remember, titles begin with a capital letter.

1. ms. Earhart lived an exciting life.

   _____

2. Her husband, mr. George Putnam, printed a book about her last
   journey.

   _____

   _____

3. grandpa Leo gave aunt Sonia the book.

   _____

4. grandma Lucy read it last year.

   _____

5. She also read a book about mrs. Roosevelt.

   _____

Try It

What person from history would you like to meet? Use the person's
title in your answer.

_____

_____

Lesson 2.4 Capitalizing Place Names

The **names of special places** always begin with a capital letter.

Ⓡockwell Ⓔlementary Ⓢchool   Ⓖarner Ⓢcience Ⓜuseum

Ⓞrlando, Ⓕlorida   Ⓑay Ⓥillage Ⓛibrary

Ⓜississippi Ⓡiver   Ⓜars

Ⓓonovan Ⓢtreet   Ⓕrance

Complete It

Complete each sentence below with the word in parentheses ( ). Remember, special places begin with a capital letter.

1. My family left Charlotte,

    _____ (north carolina), yesterday

    morning.

2. We waved good-bye to our house on

    _____ (clancy avenue).

3. We passed _____

    (washington elementary school).

4. Then, we crossed _____

    (hilliard bridge).

5. We were on our way across the _____

    (united states)!

Lesson 2.4 Capitalizing Place Names

Proof It

Read the postcard below. Find the 15 words that should begin with a capital letter. Underline each letter that should be a capital three times (≡). Then, write the capital letter above it.

Hi Annie,

    I am writing from arizona. Today, we went to the tucson children's museum. Tomorrow, we will head to the grand canyon. Next week, we'll be in california. We will visit stanford university. That is where my parents went to college. Then, we will head north. I can't wait to see redwood national forest.

    Your pal,

      Priya

Annie Schneider

452 cherry lane

charlotte, NC 22471

Try It

1. What state or city would you like to visit? Be sure to capitalize the name in your answer.

_____

2. What school do you go to? Write your answer on the line below. Use capital letters where they are needed.

_____

Lesson 2.5 Capitalizing Days, Months, and Holidays

The **days of the week** each begin with a capital letter.

Ⓜonday, Ⓣuesday, Ⓦednesday, Ⓣhursday, Ⓕriday, Ⓢaturday, Ⓢunday

The **months of the year** are also capitalized.

Ⓙanuary, Ⓜay, Ⓙune, Ⓞctober

The **names of holidays** begin with a capital letter.

Ⓒhristmas, Ⓣhanksgiving, Ⓥalentine's Ⓓay, Ⓚwanzaa

Proof It

Read the sentences below. Underline each letter that should be a capital three times (≡). Then, write the capital letter above it.

1. I have to go to the doctor on monday.

2. Softball practice starts on tuesday afternoon.

3. wednesday is Miguel's birthday.

4. There is no school on presidents' day.

5. I will go to my piano lesson on friday.

6. We will go to the grocery store on saturday morning.

7. Grandma will visit during hanukkah.

Mon.	Tues.	Wed.	Thurs.	Fri.	Sat.	Sun.
1 doctor appointment	2 softball practice	3 Miguel's birthday	4 presidents' day	5 piano practice	6 grocery shopping	7 hanukkah

Lesson 2.5 Capitalizing Days, Months, and Holidays

Rewrite It

The Brandon family keeps a list of important holidays and dates. Read the list. If the date or holiday is written correctly, make a check mark (✓) on the line. If it is not written correctly, rewrite it.

Ella's birthday	january 20	_____
valentine's Day	February 14	_____
Shane's party	May 11	_____
Kahlil's first birthday	june 22	_____
the Cheswicks' trip	july 18	_____
thanksgiving	November 23	_____
Tyson's birthday	december 29	_____

Try It

1. Write a sentence about something that happened this week. Tell what day of the week it happened.

   _____

   _____

2. What is your favorite holiday? Why?

   _____

   _____

Lesson 2.6 Periods

Periods are used at the ends of statements and commands. They tell the reader that a sentence has ended.

We ate tomato soup for lunch.

It will probably rain this afternoon.

Run as fast as you can.

Kris was wearing a blue baseball cap.

Proof It

Read the paragraph below. It is missing six periods. Add the missing periods. Circle each one so that it is easy to see.

Tip	A capital letter can be a sign that a new sentence is beginning.

Most people do not like mosquitoes If you spend any time outside

in the summer, you will probably get bitten Not all mosquitoes bite

people Only female mosquitoes bite

people When mosquitoes bite, they take

a drop of blood from a person Some

mosquitoes like birds or flowers better

Lesson 2.6 Periods

Rewrite It

Rewrite the following sentences. Each one should end with a period.
Circle the periods.

1. There are thousands of types of mosquitoes

_____

2. Mosquitoes like human sweat

_____

3. Some people never get mosquito bites

_____

4. Mosquitoes lay eggs in still water

_____

5. Bug spray can protect you from bites

_____

Try It

Have you ever been bitten by a bug? Write two sentences about it.
Both sentences should end with a period.

_____

_____

_____

Lesson 2.7 Question Marks

Use a **question mark** to end a sentence that asks a question.

Where did you put the crayons**?**

What time will Grandpa get here**?**

How did you like the play**?**

Did you go swimming**?**

Complete It

Read each answer below. Then, write the question that goes with the answer.

Example: **Q:** <u>What color is the sweater?</u>

A: The sweater is yellow.

1. **Q:** _____

   A: I ate spaghetti for dinner.

2. **Q:** _____

   A: My skateboard is in the garage.

3. **Q:** _____

   A: Keiko went to the library.

4. **Q:** _____

   A: Ashton is seven years old.

5. **Q:** _____

   A: Mr. Arnold lives in Houston.

6. **Q:** _____

   A: The book is about a boy who wishes he could fly.

Lesson 2.7 Question Marks

Proof It

Theo is asking an author questions for a school report. Cross out the six wrong end marks. Add the correct end marks, and circle them.

Theo: What do you like about being a writer.

Ms. Loden: I love to tell stories.

Theo: Where do you get your ideas.

Ms. Loden: I used to be a teacher? Many ideas come from the children who were in my classes.

Theo: When do you write.

Ms. Loden: I write for about four hours every morning?

Theo: Do you have any hobbies.

Ms. Loden: I like to garden, ski, and do crossword puzzles.

Try It

What are two questions you would like to ask the author of your favorite book? Write them on the lines below. Remember to end each question with a question mark.

_____

_____

_____

_____

Lesson 2.8 Exclamation Points

An **exclamation point** is used to end a sentence that is exciting. Sometimes exclamation points are used to show surprise.

Look at the rainbow**!**   I loved that movie**!**

Wow**!**   My class got a new computer**!**

Proof It

Read the poster below. Six exclamation points and two periods are missing. Add the end marks where they are needed.

Hurray

THE BELLVIEW FAIR

is coming to town in July

Win great prizes

Ride the biggest Ferris wheel
in Clark County

Sample tasty foods
from around the world

Admission is $3.00 for adults
and $2.00 for kids under twelve

The fair opens July 6 and closes July 12

DON'T MISS ALL THE FUN

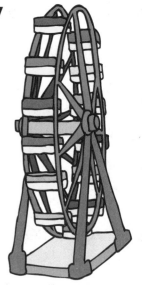

Lesson 2.8 Exclamation Points

Complete It

Read the sentences below. One sentence in each pair should end with a period. One should end with an exclamation point. Add the correct end marks.

1. I went to the Bellview Fair__
   I had the best time__

2. I played a game called Toss the Ring__
   I won four stuffed animals__

3. All the sheep escaped from their pen__
   It did not take the farmers long to catch them, though__

4. I ate a snow cone and some cotton candy__
   The cotton candy got stuck in my hair__

Try It

Think about an exciting place you have been. It could be a fair, sports event, field trip, or vacation. Write two exciting things that happened. End each sentence with an exclamation point.

Example: Yea, he hit a homerun!   Wow, what a game!

_____

_____

_____

_____

Lesson 2.9 Periods in Abbreviations

An **abbreviation** is a short way of writing something. Most abbreviations are followed by a period.

The **days of the week** can be abbreviated.

Mon. Tues. Wed. Thurs. Fri. Sat. Sun.

The **months of the year** also can be abbreviated. **May, June,** and **July** are not abbreviated because their names are so short.

Jan. Feb. Mar. Apr. Aug. Sept. Oct. Nov. Dec.

People's titles are almost always abbreviated when they come before a name.

Mrs. = mistress   Mr. = mister   Dr. = doctor

Types of streets are abbreviated in addresses.

St. = street   Ave. = avenue   Dr. = drive   Ln. = lane

Match It

Read each underlined word in the first column. Find the matching abbreviation in the second column. Write the letter of the abbreviation on the line.

1. _____ 19052 Inglewood <u>Avenue</u>	**a.**	Thurs.
2. _____ <u>Doctor</u> Weinstein	**b.**	Jan.
3. _____ <u>Thursday</u> night	**c.**	Dr.
4. _____ <u>October</u> 15, 2006	**d.**	Ln.
5. _____ 18 Winding Creek <u>Lane</u>	**e.**	Ave.
6. _____ <u>January</u> 1, 2000	**f.**	Oct.

Lesson 2.9 Periods in Abbreviations

Complete It

Read each word in parentheses ( ). Write the abbreviation.

Example: Sunday, _____ Nov. _____ (November) 12

1. 4250 Rosehill _____ (Street)

2. _____ (Mister) Ortega

3. _____ (April) 4, 2014

4. _____ (February) 10, 1904

5. _____ (Wednesday) morning

6. _____ (Mistress) Antonivic

7. Beech _____ (Drive)

Try It

1. Write your street address or school address using an abbreviation. Here are some other abbreviations you may need:

   Rd. = road   Blvd. = boulevard   Ct. = court   Cir. = circle

   _____

2. Write today's date using an abbreviation for the day of the week and month.

   _____

Lesson 2.10 Commas with Dates, Cities, and States

Commas are used in dates. They are used in between the day of the month and the year.

January 11, 1988   October 8, 1845   June 25, 2015

Commas are also used in between the names of cities and states.

Charleston, South Carolina   Bangor, Maine

When the names of cities and states are in the middle of a sentence, a comma goes after the name of the state, too.

After we left Council Bluffs, Iowa, we headed north.
Meghan and Becca moved from Oxford, Ohio, to San Antonio, Texas.

Proof It

Read the words below. Eight commas are missing. Add each comma where it belongs by using this symbol (∧).

Example: Once you pass Huntsville ∧ Alabama ∧ you will be halfway there.

1. Selma was born on August 16 2008.

2. She lives in Taos New Mexico.

3. Her little sister was born on April 4 2012.

4. Selma's grandparents live in Denver Colorado.

5. It is a long drive from Denver Colorado to Taos New Mexico.

6. The last time Selma's grandparents visited was December 20 2013.

Lesson 2.10 Commas with Dates, Cities, and States

Baltimore

Identify It

Read each line below. If it is correct, make a check mark (✓) on the line. If it is wrong, rewrite it.

1. March, 4 1952 _____

2. Butte Montana _____

3. May 27 2001 _____

4. The plane stopped in Baltimore, Maryland, to get more fuel.

_____

5. It snowed eight inches in Stowe Vermont.

_____

6. November 4, 2015 _____

7. Gum Spring, Virginia is where my grandma lives.

_____

Try It

1. Write a sentence about a city and state you would like to visit. Remember to use commas where they are needed.

_____

2. Ask a classmate when he or she was born. Write the date, including the year, on the line below.

_____

Lesson 2.11 Commas in Series and in Letters

A **series** is a list of words. Use a comma after each word in the series except the last word.

Mom bought carrots, lettuce, tomatoes, and peppers.
Cody's sisters are named Cassidy, Cameron, Casey, and Colleen.

In a letter, a comma follows **the greeting** and **the closing**.
Dear Mr. Wong,   Your friend,

Rewrite It

Rewrite the sentences below. Add commas to each list to make the sentences clearer.

1. Mom got out the picnic basket the plates and the cups.

   _____

   _____

2. Lily packed forks knives spoons and napkins.

   _____

   _____

3. Amelia added pears oranges and apples.

   _____

4. Dad made sandwiches a salad and brownies.

   _____

   _____

Lesson 2.11 Commas in Series and in Letters

Proof It

Read the letter below. Ten commas are missing. Add each comma where it belongs by using this symbol (∧).

Dear Grandma

    Yesterday, we went to the park. Lily Amelia and Mom shook out the picnic blanket. Dad carried the basket the drinks and the toys from the car. We all ate some salad a sandwich and a fruit.

    Deepak Sita and Raj were at the park with their parents, too. We played tag and fed the ducks. Later, we shared our brownies with the Nair family. I wish you could have been there!

    Love

    Max

Try It

1. Imagine you were going on a picnic. What three things would you bring with you? Remember to separate the things in your list with commas.

    _____

    _____

2. Name three people who live on your street or go to your school. Separate their names with commas.

    _____

    _____

Lesson 2.12 Commas in Compound Sentences

A **compound sentence** is made up of two smaller sentences. The smaller sentences are joined by a comma and the word **and** or **but**.

Michelle went to the store.   She bought some markers.
Michelle went to the store**, and** she bought some markers.

Bats sleep during the day.   They are active at night.
Bats sleep during the day**, but** they are active at night.

Rewrite It

Read the sentences below. Combine them using a comma and the word **and** or **but**.

1. Abby rode her bike. Gilbert rode his scooter.

   _____

   _____

2. My new bedroom is big. My old bedroom was cozy.

   _____

   _____

3. The black cat is beautiful. The orange cat is friendly.

   _____

   _____

4. Roberto is quick. Sophie is more graceful.

   _____

Lesson 2.12 Commas in Compound Sentences

Proof It

Read the paragraph below. Four commas are missing from compound sentences. Add each comma where it belongs by using this symbol (∧).

Tip	Look for the words **and** or **but**. Ask yourself if they join two complete sentences.

The leaves of the poison ivy plant are shaped like almonds and they come in groups of three. Poison ivy can cause a rash and it can make you itch. The leaves of the plant contain oil that causes the rash. Some people can touch the plant but they will not get a rash.

The oil can stick to your clothes. Washing with soap and water can get rid of the oil and it can keep the rash from spreading.

Try It

Write a compound sentence about what you like to do and what a friend of yours likes to do. Remember to join the two parts of your sentence with a comma and the word **and** or **but**.

Example: I like to play at the park, and Deena likes to go swimming.

_____

_____

Lesson 2.13 Apostrophes in Possessives

When something belongs to a person or thing, they own it. An apostrophe and the letter **s** ('s) at the end of a word show that the person or thing is the owner.

the car**'s** engine   Stacy**'s** eyes

Jake**'s** laugh   the table**'s** leg

Rewrite It

Read each phrase below. Then, rewrite it on the line as a possessive.

Example: the coat of Kayla _____ Kayla's coat _____

1. the roar of the lion _____

2. the spots of the leopard _____

3. the trip of Amy _____

4. the lens of the camera _____

5. the hat of Tim _____

6. the roof of the jeep _____

Lesson 2.13 Apostrophes in Possessives

Match It

Read the words below. Then, read the answer choices. Write the letter of your answer on the line.

1. _____ the horn of the rhino
   a. the rhino's horn   b. the horn's rhino

2. _____ the animals of Africa
   a. the animal's of Africa   b. Africa's animals

3. _____ the photos of John
   a. John photo's   b. John's photos

4. _____ the leader of the safari
   a. the safari's leader   b. the leader safari's

5. _____ the favorite animal of Don
   a. Don's favorite animal's   b. Don's favorite animal

6. _____ the baby of the hippo
   a. the baby's hippo   b. the hippo's baby

7. _____ the tent of Sarah
   a. Sarah's tent   b. Sarah tent

Try It

1. On the line below, write something you like about one of your friends. Use the possessive form of your friend's name.

   Example: I like William's smile.

   _____

Lesson 2.14 Quotation Marks in Dialogue

Quotation marks are used around the exact words a person says. One set of quotation marks is used before the first word the person says. Another set is used at the end of the person's words.

> Jamal said, "I am going to play in a piano recital on Saturday."
> "Do you like fresh apple pie?" asked the baker.
> "Hurray!" shouted Sydney. "Today is a snow day!"

Remember to put the second pair of quotation marks after the punctuation mark that ends the sentence.

Complete It

Read each sentence below. Underline the speaker's exact words. Then, add a set of quotation marks before and after the speaker's words.

Example: Enzo shouted, "Catch the ball, Katie!"

1. Would you like to go to skiing this afternoon? asked Mom.

2. Alyssa asked, Where will we go?

3. Mom said, Wintergreen Mountain is not too far away.

4. Can I bring a friend? asked Zane.

5. Mom said, You can each bring along one friend.

6. Alyssa said, Riley will be so excited!

Tip	The exact words people say are sometimes called **dialogue**. Quotation marks are used to show which words are dialogue.

Lesson 2.14 Quotation Marks in Dialogue

Rewrite It

Read each sentence below. Write the sentence again. Add quotation marks where they are needed. Remember to find the speaker's exact words first.

1. Have you ever been skiing? Zane asked his friend.

   _____

2. Joey said, No, but it sounds like fun.

   _____

3. Riley said, My grandpa taught me how to ski.

   _____

4. She added, He lives near the mountains in Vermont.

   _____

   _____

Try It

Write two sentences that have people speaking. Begin each sentence with one of these phrases.

   My mom said, My friend said, My sister said, My grandpa said,

1. _____

2. _____

Lesson 2.15 Titles of Books and Movies

The **titles of books and movies** are underlined in text. This lets the reader know that the underlined words are part of a title.

Cristina's favorite movie is <u>Because of Winn-Dixie</u>.

Harry wrote a book report on <u>Nate the Great and the Musical Note</u>.

Roald Dahl is the author of <u>James and the Giant Peach</u>.

I have seen the movie <u>Aladdin</u> four times.

Rewrite It

Read the sentences below. Rewrite each sentence and underline the title of each movie.

1. Tom Hanks was the voice of Woody in the movie Toy Story.

   _____

2. Mara Wilson played Matilda Wormwood in the movie Matilda.

   _____

3. In the movie Shrek, Cameron Diaz was the voice of Princess Fiona.

   _____

4. The movie Fly Away Home is based on a true story.

   _____

5. Harriet the Spy is the name of a book and a movie.

   _____

Lesson 2.15 Titles of Books and Movies

Proof It

Read the paragraphs below. Find the five book titles and underline them.

Jon Scieszka (say **shez ka**) is a popular author. He has written many books for children. He is best known for his book The Stinky Cheese Man and Other Fairly Stupid Tales. Jon has always loved books. Dr. Seuss's famous book Green Eggs and Ham made Jon feel like he could be a writer one day.

In 1989, Jon wrote The True Story of the Three Little Pigs. Many children think his books are very funny. They also like the pictures. Lane Smith draws the pictures for many of Jon's books. They worked together on the book Math Curse. Their book Science Verse is also popular.

Try It

1. Write the title of your favorite book on the line below. Remember to underline it.

   _____

   _____

2. What was the last movie you saw? Write the title on the line below. Remember to underline it.

   _____

   _____

Lesson 3.1 Subject-Verb Agreement (Adding **s**)

When there is only one person or thing, add **s** to the end of an action verb.

    <u>Caleb</u> run**s** to the park.   <u>Ms. Wheeler</u> read**s** to us every day.

An action verb does not end with **s** when there is more than one person or thing, or when using **you**.

    <u>The balloons</u> float through the air.   <u>You</u> pull the string.

Complete It

Read each sentence below. Then, read the pair of verbs in parentheses ( ). Choose the correct verb form. Write it on the line.

1. Wade _____ a game for the family. (pick, picks)

2. He _____ the wheel. (spin, spins)

3. Wade _____ a picture on a big sheet of paper. (draw, draws)

4. Mom and Dad _____. (laugh, laughs)

5. Alicia _____ what the picture is. (know, knows)

6. She _____ the bell. (ring, rings)

7. Alicia and Wade _____ a good team. (make, makes)

Lesson 3.1 Subject-Verb Agreement (Adding **s**)

Proof It

Read each sentence below. Add an **s** to the end of the verb if needed.

1. The Andersons love__ game night.

2. Alicia choose__ the game.

3. She pick__ her favorite board game.

4. Mom, Dad, Alicia, and Wade roll__ the dice.

5. Wade take__ the first turn.

6. He move__ his piece four spaces.

7. Mom roll__ the dice.

8. Uh-oh! Mom lose__ her turn.

9. Mom never win__ this game!

Try It

Use a pair of verbs from the box to write two sentences. One sentence should have only one person or thing. The other sentence should have more than one person or thing.

run, runs	play, plays
smile, smiles	throw, throws

1. _____

2. _____

Lesson 3.2 Subject-Verb Agreement (Adding **es**)

Sometimes, **es** needs to be added instead of just **s**. Add **es** to verbs that end in **sh**, **ch**, **s**, **x**, and **z**.

Ellie brush**es** her hair before she goes to bed.

Grandma stitch**es** the letters on the pillow.

He miss**es** his old house.

When there is more than one person or thing, verbs do not end in **s** or **es**.

Complete It

Read the sentences below. Choose the correct verb at the end of each sentence. Write it on the blank.

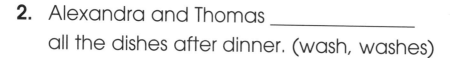

1. The bee _____ when it flies close to my ear. (buzz, buzzes)

2. Alexandra and Thomas _____ all the dishes after dinner. (wash, washes)

3. Manuel _____ the ball to Ashley. (toss, tosses)

4. Noelle _____ for something special when she blows out her candles. (wish, wishes)

5. Liam _____ the batter before he pours it in the pan. (mix, mixes)

Lesson 3.2 Subject-Verb Agreement (Adding **es**)

Solve It

Circle the verb in each sentence below. If it is correct, make a check mark (✓) on the line. If it is not correct, write the correct form. Then, see if you can find each verb in the word search puzzle. Circle the verbs you find in the puzzle. Words can be found across and down.

1. Mom and Dad relaxes on the weekends. _____

2. The snake hisses at the bird. _____

3. Liza catch the bus each morning. _____

4. Sean waxes his surfboard on the beach. _____

5. The red sports car pass the truck. _____

r	e	l	a	x	o	h	k
w	d	j	u	t	c	i	q
a	p	a	s	s	e	s	c
x	g	j	b	b	o	s	w
e	c	a	t	c	h	e	s
s	e	h	k	u	l	s	y

Try It

Write two sentences. Correctly use a verb from the box in each sentence.

touch	misses
fixes	push
rush	crashes

1. _____

   _____

2. _____

   _____

Lesson 3.3 Irregular Verbs: **Am**, **Is**, **Are**

Some verbs to do not show action. The verb **to be** does not show action. **Am**, **is**, and **are** are all different forms of the verb **to be**.

Am is used only with **I**.

I **am** happy.   I **am** behind the door.

Is is used when there is only one person or thing.

Tommy **is** my brother.   The sky **is** blue.

Are is used with **you**.

You **are** lucky.   You **are** my friend.

Are is also used when there is more than one person or thing.

Blanca and Charley **are** at school.   They **are** in second grade.

Complete It

Read each sentence below. Choose the correct verb from the parentheses ( ). Write it on the line.

1. I _____ tall and strong. (is, am)

2. You _____ a great cook. (are, am)

3. Gavin and Mitch _____ twins. (is, are)

4. This soup _____ too spicy! (is, am)

5. I _____ a niece. (are, am)

6. All the girls in my class _____ excited. (is, are)

7. That skateboard _____ broken. (are, is)

NAME _____

Lesson 3.3 Irregular Verbs: **Am, Is, Are**

Proof It

Read the diary entry below. The wrong forms of the verbs **am**, **is**, and **are** are used. Cross out each incorrect verb in bold type. Then, write the correct form above it.

Thursday, May 27

Dear Diary,

Victoria **are** my friend. She knows lots of jokes. Today, I told her, "You **am** the funniest person I know! I **are** glad to be your friend."

We **is** in a club together. Owen and Rachel **is** in the club, too. We learn all kinds of jokes. Knock-knock jokes **is** my favorite.

Riddles **am** Victoria's favorite.

Owen **are** older than us. He **am** in third grade. He tells us all the third-grade jokes. We spend a lot of time laughing!

Try It

1. Write a sentence with only one person or thing. Use **is**.

   _____

2. Write a sentence with more than one person or thing. Use **are**.

   _____

Lesson 3.4 Irregular Verbs: **Has**, **Have**

Some verbs do not show action. The verb **to have** does not show action. **Has** and **have** are different forms of the verb **to have**.

Have is used with **I** or **you**.

<u>I</u> **have** six cats.   <u>You</u> **have** a bird.

Have is also used when there is more than one person or thing.
<u>We</u> **have** a French lesson this afternoon.
<u>They</u> **have** a green car.
<u>Maureen and Ramon</u> **have** brown hair.
<u>The tree and the plant</u> **have** leaves.

Has is used when there is only one person or thing.
<u>She</u> **has** two braids.   <u>Lex</u> **has** a book about fossils.
<u>The moon</u> **has** a rough surface.

Complete It

Read each sentence below. Then, read the pair of verbs in parentheses. Choose the correct verb form and write it on the line.

1. Maple trees and oak trees _____ similar leaves. (has, have)

2. A gingko tree _____ leaves that look like fans. (has, have)

3. We _____ a large fir tree in the backyard. (has, have)

4. The Maddens _____ many trees that bloom in the spring. (has, have)

5. Lila _____ an enormous, old maple tree in the front yard. (has, have)

Lesson 3.4 Irregular Verbs: **Has, Have**

Proof It

There is a mistake with the verb in each sentence below. Cross out the incorrect verb. Then, write the correct verb above it.

1. Holly trees has shiny red berries.

2. You has a beautiful weeping willow tree.

3. An apple tree have plenty of fruit in autumn.

4. A mulberry tree have berries that birds love to eat.

5. Jaya and Chad has a swing in the old oak tree.

6. I has a piece of bark from the white birch tree.

7. Sparrows and chickadees has a nest in the elm tree.

Try It

1. Write a sentence about something you have.

_____

_____

2. Write a sentence about something one of your friends has.

_____

_____

Lesson 3.5 Forming the Past Tense by Adding **ed**

Verbs in the **present tense** tell about things that are happening right now. Verbs in the **past tense** tell about things that already happened. Add **ed** to most verbs to tell about the past.

Teresa jump**ed** over the log. Grandma push**ed** the stroller.
The tall boy kick**ed** the ball. Mr. Tisdall talk**ed** to the class.

If the verb already ends in **e**, just add **d**.

The family hik**ed** two miles. (hik**e**)

She plac**ed** the cups on the table. (plac**e**)

Complete It

The sentences below are missing verbs. Complete each sentence with the past tense of the verb in parentheses ( ).

1. Annie Smith Peck _____ to many countries. (travel)

2. In 1888, she _____ Mount Shasta in California. (climb)

3. She _____ to climb the Matterhorn one day. (hope)

4. Annie _____ a group called the American Alpine Club. (start)

5. She _____ the volcanoes of South America. (explore)

6. She _____ hard so she could climb in her spare time. (work)

7. Annie _____ climbing until she was 82. (continue)

Lesson 3.5 Forming the Past Tense by Adding **ed**

Rewrite It

Rewrite the sentences below in the past tense by adding **ed** to the underlined verb. If the verb already ends in **e**, just add **d** to change it to the past tense.

Example: Darby <u>pull</u> on his leash.   Darby **pulled** on his leash.

1. Annie Smith Peck <u>climb</u> many mountains.

   _____

2. She <u>live</u> from 1850 until 1935.

   _____

3. Annie <u>show</u> the world how strong women can be.

   _____

4. She <u>want</u> to set records in climbing.

   _____

Try It

Write two sentences about what you did last week. Make sure the verbs are in the past tense.

1. _____

   _____

2. _____

   _____

Lesson 3.6 Past-Tense Verbs: **Was, Were**

The past tense of **am** and **is** is **was**. Remember to use **was** only if there is one person or thing.

I **was** tired.   The house **was** white.

The past tense of **are** is **were**. Remember to use **were** if there is more than one person or thing.

We **were** a team.   The monkeys **were** funny.

Complete It

Write the correct past-tense verb in the blanks below. Use **was** or **were**.

Last Tuesday, my brother Benjamin _____ on TV. He

_____ at the park with his friend Allison. It _____ a sunny

day. They _____ on the jungle gym. A news reporter _____

at the park, too. She _____ a reporter for Channel WBVA news.

She asked people in the park if the city

should build a new pool. Benjamin and

Allison _____ excited about the

interview. My family watched Benjamin

on the evening news. I _____ proud

of my brother, the TV star!

Lesson 3.6 Past-Tense Verbs: **Was, Were**

Rewrite It

The sentences below are in the present tense. Rewrite them in the past tense.

Example: The basketball <u>is</u> in the gym. The basketball was in the gym.

1. Benjamin <u>is</u> worried we would miss the news.

    _____

    _____

2. Mom and Dad <u>are</u> happy to see Ben's good manners.

    _____

    _____

3. I <u>am</u> glad Ben wore the hat I gave him.

    _____

4. You <u>are</u> on vacation.

    _____

Try It

1. Write a sentence about something that is happening right now. Use the verb **is** in your sentence.

    _____

2. Now, write the same sentence in the past tense.

    _____

Lesson 3.7 Past-Tense Verbs: **Had**

The past tense of **have** and **has** is **had**.

<u>Present Tense</u>

I **have** four pets.

The flowers **have** red petals.

Hayden **has** short hair.

<u>Past Tense</u>

I **had** four pets.

The flowers **had** red petals.

Hayden **had** short hair.

Complete It

Complete each sentence with the correct form of the verb **have**. The word in parentheses ( ) will tell you to use the present tense or the past tense.

1. My bike _____ a horn and a scoop seat. (present)

2. My mom _____ a bike just like it when she was little. (past)

3. The wheels _____ shiny silver spokes. (present)

4. My mom's old bike _____ a bell, too. (past)

Lesson 3.7 Past-Tense Verbs: **Had**

Identify It

Read each sentence below. Circle the verb. If the sentence is in the present tense, write **pres**. in the space. If it is in the past tense, write **past**.

1. _____ The one-dollar bill has a picture of George Washington on it.

2. _____ I had four dollars in my piggybank.

3. _____ The twenty-dollar bill has a picture of Andrew Jackson on it.

4. _____ Greg and Devi had ten dollars to spend at the bookstore.

5. _____ My sister has eight dollars.

6. _____ My parents have a can collection.

7. _____ Ian had a two-dollar bill.

Try It

1. Write a sentence about something you have.

   _____

2. Now, rewrite your sentence in the past tense.

   _____

Lesson 3.8 Past-Tense Verbs: **Went**

The past tense of the verb **go** is **went**.

Present Tense
We **go** to the fair with
our cousins.
Lorenzo **goes** to Florida.

Past Tense
We **went** to the fair with our
cousins.
Lorenzo **went** to Florida.

Rewrite It

Rewrite each sentence in the past tense.

1. We <u>go</u> to the store.

   _____

2. Trish <u>goes</u> to her singing lesson on Thursday.

   _____

3. Sanjay <u>goes</u> home at noon.

   _____

4. We <u>go</u> sledding with Miki and Ted.

   _____

Lesson 3.8 Past-Tense Verbs: **Went**

Proof It

Some of the verbs below are in the wrong tense. Cross out the underlined verbs. Write the correct past-tense verbs above them.

When my dad was little, his family <u>goes</u> to a cabin every summer. He loved the little cabin in the woods. His cousins came to visit. Everyone <u>goes</u> swimming in the lake. They <u>go</u> on long bike rides. They built forts in the woods. Grandma and Grandpa <u>go</u> for long walks. Once the entire family came from miles away. They <u>go</u> to a big family party on the beach.

Dad loved those summers in the woods. Some day, he will take us to see the old cabin.

Try It

1. Write a sentence using the verb **go** or **goes**.

_____

_____

2. Now, rewrite your sentence in the past tense.

_____

_____

Lesson 3.9 Past-Tense Verbs: **Saw**

The past tense of the verb **see** is **saw**.

Present Tense
My mom **sees** me swimming.
Franco and Ana **see** the
   puppy every day.

Past Tense
My mom **saw** me swimming.
Franco and Ana **saw** the
   puppy every day.

Rewrite It

Rewrite each sentence in the past tense.

1. We <u>see</u> raindrops on the leaves.

   _____

2. The dragon <u>sees</u> the little girl climbing the hill.

   _____

3. Dad <u>sees</u> the tiny cut when he put on his glasses.

   _____

4. The three birds <u>see</u> their mother.

   _____

5. Tess <u>sees</u> that movie three times.

   _____

6. Cameron and Dillon <u>see</u> the hot air balloon.

   _____

Lesson 3.9 Past-Tense Verbs: **Saw**

Proof It

Some of the verbs below are in the wrong tense. Cross out the underlined verbs. Write the correct past-tense verbs above them.

My aunt got married in Key West, Florida.

We <u>see</u> many interesting things on our visit.

My sister <u>sees</u> dolphins playing in the water. Dad took us to Ripley's

Believe It or Not Museum. We <u>see</u> many strange and amazing things

there. Later, we went to the Chicken Store. It is a place that rescues

chickens. We <u>see</u> dozens of chickens there. I did not know Key West

had so many homeless chickens!

Try It

1. What is the first thing you see when you wake up in the morning? Write your answer in the past tense.

   _____

   _____

2. What is the first thing you see when you go to school? Write your answer in the past tense.

   _____

   _____

Lesson 3.10 Contractions with **Not**

A **contraction** is a short way of saying something. In a contraction, two words are joined. An apostrophe (') goes in place of the missing letters.

Many contractions are formed with the word **not**. The apostrophe takes the place of the letter **o** in **not**.

is not = isn't	are not = aren't
was not = wasn't	were not = weren't
does not = doesn't	did not = didn't
have not = haven't	can not = can't

Match It

Match each pair of underlined words with its contraction. Write the letter of the contraction in the space.

1. _____ The cat and the mouse <u>are not</u> friends. **a.** can't

2. _____ They <u>can not</u> get along. **b.** isn't

3. _____ They <u>have not</u> tried very hard, though. **c.** wasn't

4. _____ The cat <u>was not</u> friendly to the mouse. **d.** weren't

5. _____ The mouse <u>is not</u> kind to the cat. **e.** aren't

6. _____ I guess the cat and mouse <u>were not</u> meant **f.** haven't
   to live happily ever after.

Lesson 3.10 Contractions with **Not**

Rewrite It

Circle the two words in each sentence you
could combine to make a contraction. Then,
write the sentences using contractions.

1. Mr. Irving Mouse can not come out during the day.

   _____

2. He does not want to run into Miss Lola Cat.

   _____

3. Being chased is not Irving's idea of a good time.

   _____

4. He did not think Lola would be so rude.

   _____

5. They are not going to be able to share this house.

   _____

Try It

1. Write a sentence using one of the following pairs of words: **is not**,
   are not, **did not**, or **have not**

   _____

2. Now, rewrite your sentence using a contraction.

   _____

Lesson 3.11 Contractions with **Am**, **Is**, **Are**

Some contractions are formed with the words **am**, **is**, and **are**. The apostrophe takes the place of the letter **a** in **am**. It takes the place of **i** in **is**. It takes the place of **a** in **are**.

I am = I'm   you are = you're

we are = we're   they are = they're

it is = it's   he is = he's

she is = she's

Proof It

Read the diary entry below. Draw a line through the words in bold type. Then, write the contractions above the words.

Dear Diary,

    I am going to my karate class on Saturday morning. **It is** a class for beginners. Maria and Toby are taking karate, too. **They are** in my class. Maria learned some karate moves from her older brother. **He is** in a different class. Maria knows how to do more kicks than anyone else. I think **she is** the best student. Allan is our karate teacher. **He is** 39 years old. He has been doing karate since he was five. He has a black belt. Maria, Toby, and I plan to take lessons for a long time. **We are** going to get our black belts one day, too.

Lesson 3.11 Contractions with **Am**, **Is**, **Are**

Complete It

Fill in the blanks below with a contraction from the box.

It's	You're	He's
We're	She's	They're

1. I think Allan is a great teacher. _____ patient and funny.

2. Maria's mom comes to every class. _____ interested in what we learn.

3. Toby and Maria are cousins. _____ both part of the Tarrano family.

4. Maria, Toby, and I will get our yellow belts next month. _____ excited to move up a level.

5. I like karate class a lot. _____ a good way to exercise and make friends.

6. Do you think you would like to try karate? _____ welcome to come watch one of our classes.

Try It

1. Write a sentence using the contraction for **she is**.

   _____

2. Write a sentence using the contraction for **they are**.

   _____

Lesson 3.12 Contractions with **Will**

Many contractions are formed with pronouns and the verb **will**. An apostrophe (') takes the place of the letters **wi** in **will**.

I will = I'll   it will = it'll
you will = you'll   we will = we'll
she will = she'll   they will = they'll
he will = he'll

Match It

Match each pair of underlined words with its contraction. Write the letter of the contraction in the space.

1. _____ I will travel into space one day.   **a.** She'll

2. _____ A spaceship will take me there. It will move very fast.   **b.** We'll

3. _____ You will be my co-pilot.   **c.** I'll

4. _____ My sister, Eva, can come along, too. She will direct the spaceship.   **d.** They'll

5. _____ We will make many important discoveries.   **e.** You'll

6. _____ Our families can have a party when we return. They will be so proud!   **f.** It'll

Lesson 3.12 Contractions with **Will**

Proof It

Read the newspaper article below. Draw a line through the underlined words. Then, write the contractions above the words.

Hughes to Become Youngest Astronaut

Jasmine Hughes is only nine years old. <u>She will</u> be the first child to journey into space. Jasmine has been training since she was four. <u>She will</u> travel on the spaceship Investigator. Six other astronauts will be in her crew. <u>They will</u> have to work well as a team. Darren Unger will be the commander. <u>He will</u> be the leader of the crew. They know their mission is important. <u>It will</u> help scientists learn more about the universe. The world will be able to watch parts of the trip on TV. <u>We will</u> see history being made!

Try It

1. Write a sentence using the contraction for **he will**.

   _____

   _____

2. Write a sentence using the contraction for **I will**.

   _____

   _____

Lesson 3.13 Plural Nouns with **s**

The word **plural** means **more than one**. To make most nouns plural, just add **s**.

one clock → two clock**s**   one shirt → three shirt**s**

one girl → many girl**s**   one squirrel → six squirrel**s**

Complete It

Read the sentences below. Complete each sentence with the plural form of the word in parentheses ( ).

Example: The _____boys_____ played tag until it got dark outside. (boy)

1. There are five blue _____ on Greece's flag. (stripe)

2. China's flag has five _____. (star)

3. The two _____ in Denmark's flag are red and white. (color)

4. Some flags have small _____ on them. (picture)

5. Jamaica's flag has four _____. (triangle)

6. _____ are on the flags of many countries. (Moon)

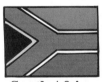
South Africa

Spain

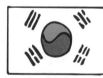
South Korea

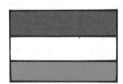
Yugoslavia

Vietnam

Sweden

Switzerland

Taiwan

Tanzania

Trinidad

Lesson 3.13 Plural Nouns with s

Solve It

The words below are all things that are on state flags of the United States. Write the plural form of each word on the line. Then, fill in the crossword puzzle using the numbers and the plural clues.

Down

1. date _____

2. bird _____

3. flower _____

5. tree _____

Across

4. animal _____

6. word _____

7. star _____

Try It

Write two sentences below. Use the plural form of at least one word from the box in each sentence.

paint	pencil	paintbrush
book	folder	pen
crayon	notebook	color

1. _____

2. _____

Lesson 3.14 Plural Nouns with **es**

If a noun ends in **sh**, **ch**, **s**, or **x**, add **es** to make it plural.

one ax → two ax**es**   one brush → many brush**es**

one pouch → six pouch**es**   one bus → seven bus**es**

Rewrite It

Read the sentences below. Then, write
the sentences with the plural form of the
underlined words.

1. There are two <u>bunch</u> of grapes on the table.

   _____

   _____

2. The <u>peach</u> are in the basket.

   _____

3. Use the <u>box</u> to carry the oranges.

   _____

4. Please put the fruit in the yellow <u>dish</u>.

   _____

   _____

5. Each of the <u>class</u> will get to pick some berries.

   _____

   _____

Lesson 3.14 Plural Nouns with es

Proof It

Read the paragraphs below. The underlined words should be plural. To make a word plural, make a caret (^) at the end of the word. Then, write the letter or letters you want to add above the caret.

Example: There are three **watch**^es in the glass case.

We waited on the <u>bench</u> outside the school. The <u>bus</u> picked us up at nine o'clock. We went to Sunnyvale Apple Orchard. Mr. Krup gave us some <u>box</u> to use. He showed us how to pick ripe apples. Many <u>branch</u> were heavy with fruit. There were also some blueberry <u>bush</u> on the farm.

When we were done picking, the tractor brought us back to the farmhouse. We ate our <u>lunch</u> at some picnic tables. Mrs. Krup gave us <u>glass</u> of lemonade. Tomorrow, we'll make apple pies.

Try It

Write two sentences below. Use the plural form of at least one word from the box in each sentence.

fox	**watch**
beach	**brush**

1. _____

2. _____

Lesson 3.15 Irregular Plural Nouns

Some plural nouns do not follow the rules you have learned. To form the plurals of these nouns, do not add **s** or **es**. Instead, the whole word changes. Here are some examples.

one **man** → three **men**   one **foot** → two **feet**

one **woman** → eight **women**   one **goose** → four **geese**

one **child** → a few **children**   one **tooth** → many **teeth**

one **mouse** → twenty **mice**

Some nouns do not change at all in their plural forms.

one **deer** → many **deer**   one **moose** → nine **moose**

one **fish** → sixty **fish**   one **sheep** → one hundred **sheep**

Match It

Read the phrases in Column 1. Then, draw a line to match each phrase to its plural in Column 2.

Column 1	Column 2
one tooth	nine deer
one child	four feet
one foot	twelve mice
one goose	several teeth
one deer	lots of children
one mouse	two men
one man	seven geese

Lesson 3.15 Irregular Plural Nouns

Solve It

Write the plural form of each word on the line. Then, see if you can find each plural word in the word search puzzle. Circle the words you find in the puzzle. Words can be found across and down.

1. woman _____

2. fish _____

3. moose _____

4. mouse _____

5. foot _____

6. sheep _____

7. child _____

8. tooth _____

n	l	m	i	h	l	f	g	c	q
c	h	i	l	d	r	e	n	b	u
n	t	c	t	l	w	e	i	h	x
s	h	e	e	p	o	t	v	k	m
f	s	a	e	k	m	o	o	s	e
e	r	h	t	g	e	d	f	z	p
f	i	s	h	j	n	p	u	g	j

Try It

Write two sentences below. Use the plural form of at least one word from the box in each sentence.

foot	mouse
man	deer
fish	goose

1. _____

2. _____

Lesson 3.16 Pronouns **I** and **Me**

I and **me** are both pronouns. **Pronouns** are words that take the places of nouns. The pronouns **I** and **me** are used when the writer is talking about himself or herself.

> **I** took the bus downtown. **I** bought a sandwich. The police officer waved to **me**. **I** walked to the museum. The woman behind the desk gave **me** a ticket.

When you are talking about yourself and another person, always put the other person first.

> **Robyn and I** left early.
> He gave the shells to **Dexter and me**.

Complete It

Complete each sentence below with the pronoun **I** or **me**. Write the pronoun in the space.

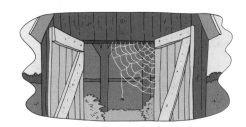

1. _____ was born in New York in 1899.

2. My five brothers and sisters were older than _____.

3. My wife and _____ moved to a farm in Maine.

4. _____ loved to read, write, and do chores on the farm.

5. A spider in my barn gave _____ the idea for a children's story.

Do you know who the mystery person is? It is E. B. White, the famous author of the books <u>Charlotte's Web</u> and <u>Stuart Little</u>.

Lesson 3.16 Pronouns **I** and **Me**

Proof It

Read the sentences below. If the correct pronoun is used, put a check mark on the line. If it is not, write the correct pronoun on the line.

1. _____ Me went to the store yesterday.

2. _____ Chris and I are on the same baseball team.

3. _____ Is that package for I?

4. _____ My sister and me are going to the playground.

5. _____ I had a great time last year at the museum.

6. _____ Running is good for I.

7. _____ Dad and me took the subway downtown.

8. _____ Amina gave I an invitation to the party.

Try It

On the lines below, write two sentences about things that happened to you last week. Use **I** in one sentence, and **me** in the other.

1. _____

_____

2. _____

_____

Lesson 3.17 Comparative Adjectives

Adjectives are words that describe nouns. They give the reader more information. Add **er** to an adjective to show that one thing is more than something else. Add **est** to an adjective to show that it is the most.

Rosa is tall.   Jill is tall**er**.   Bethany is tall**est**.

Identify It

Read the sentences below. Circle the correct adjective in parentheses.

1. Mount Everest is the (highest, higher) mountain.

2. The (tall, tallest) waterfall in the world is Angel Falls in Venezuela.

3. The Nile River is (longest, longer) than the Amazon River.

4. The Pacific Ocean is (deeper, deep) than the Indian Ocean.

5. It is the world's (deeper, deepest) ocean.

Lesson 3.17 Comparative Adjectives

Complete It

Fill in the spaces with the missing adjectives.

young	_____	youngest
_____	faster	fastest
dark	_____	_____
hard	harder	_____
new	_____	newest
_____	shorter	_____
small	_____	_____
kind	_____	kindest

Try It

On the lines below, write two sentences. Your sentences should compare people or things that are alike in some way.

Example: Stacey is older than Hasaan.   Val is the oldest.

1. _____

   _____

2. _____

   _____

Lesson 3.18 Synonyms

Synonyms are words that have the same, or almost the same, meanings. Synonyms can help you become a better writer. They make your writing more interesting to read. Here are some examples of synonyms.

little, tiny, small   easy, simple

begin, start   quick, fast

under, below   laugh, giggle

Match It

Match each word in the first column with its synonym in the second column. Write the letter of the synonym on the line.

1. _____ beautiful   **a.** enjoy

2. _____ boat   **b.** toss

3. _____ like   **c.** happy

4. _____ tired   **d.** ship

5. _____ grin   **e.** pal

6. _____ glad   **f.** sleepy

7. _____ friend   **g.** pretty

8. _____ throw   **h.** smile

Lesson 3.18 Synonyms

Complete It

Read the sentences below. Each underlined word has a synonym in the box. Write the synonym on the line at the end of the sentence.

giggled	**bugs**	**hop**
dad	**pick**	**liked**	**terrific**

1. Malik needed to <u>choose</u> a topic for his report. _____

2. He and his <u>father</u> sat down at the computer. _____

3. Malik <u>enjoyed</u> using the Internet for school projects.

   _____

4. All of a sudden, he had a <u>great</u> idea. _____

5. "I think I'm going to do my report on <u>insects</u>," Malik told his dad.

   _____

6. Malik and Dad watched a cartoon cricket <u>jump</u> across the computer screen. _____

7. Malik <u>laughed</u> when the cricket stopped and waved.

   _____

Try It

1. Write a sentence using a synonym for the word **small**.

   _____

2. Write a sentence using a synonym for the word **yelled**.

   _____

Lesson 3.19 Antonyms

An **antonym** is a word that means the opposite of another word. Here are some examples of antonyms.

big, little   old, young

happy, sad   first, last

right, wrong   never, always

Identify It

There are two antonyms in each sentence below. Circle each pair of antonyms.

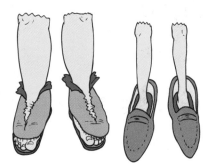

1. The tall bottle is next to the short can.

2. Kent wore his new shirt with his favorite pair of old jeans.

3. I thought the quiz would be hard, but it was easy.

4. Did Miranda smile or frown when she saw you?

5. One pair of shoes is too tight, and one pair is too loose.

6. Open the cupboard, take out the cereal, and close the door.

7. It was hot outside, but it will be cold tomorrow.

8. Stephen was the first person in line and the last person to leave.

9. Would you rather go in the morning or night?

Lesson 3.19 Antonyms

Solve It

In the spaces, write an antonym for each word below. Then, circle the antonyms in the word search puzzle. Words can be found across and down.

1. yell __ __ __ __ __ __ __

2. pull __ __ __ __

3. empty __ __ __ __

4. win __ __ __ __

5. yes __ __

6. love __ __ __ __

7. over __ __ __ __ __

8. down __ __

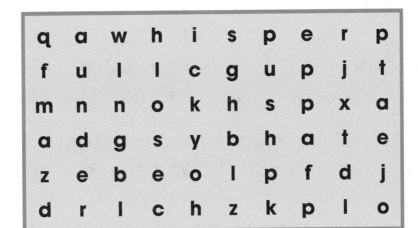

q	a	w	h	i	s	p	e	r	p
f	u	l	l	c	g	u	p	j	t
m	n	n	o	k	h	s	p	x	a
a	d	g	s	y	b	h	a	t	e
z	e	b	e	o	l	p	f	d	j
d	r	l	c	h	z	k	p	l	o

Try It

1. Write a sentence using an antonym for **loud**.

   _____

2. Write a sentence using an antonym for **soft**.

   _____

Lesson 3.20 Homophones

Homophones are words that sound alike but have different spellings and meanings. Here are some examples of homophones.

to = toward	We went **to** the gym.
OR	
use **to** with a verb	Dennis wants **to** skate.
two = the number that comes after one	Give the dog **two** biscuits.
too = also	We will go, **too**.
OR	
too = very; more than enough	Lindy is **too** young to go.
by = next to	The bag is **by** the door.
bye = good-bye	Karim waved and said **bye**.
buy = to purchase something	I will **buy** three pears.
right = the opposite of wrong	That is the **right** answer.
write = to record your words	**Write** a report about the book.

Complete It

Choose the correct word to complete each sentence. Write it on the line.

1. I would like _____ see *Pinocchio* on ice. (to, too)

2. My sister wants to go, _____. (two, too)

3. Mom said she will try to _____ tickets tonight. (bye, buy)

4. I am going to _____ about the show in my diary. (write, right)

Lesson 3.20 Homophones

Proof It

Read the poster below. There are five mistakes. Cross out each mistake. Then, write the correct homophone above it.

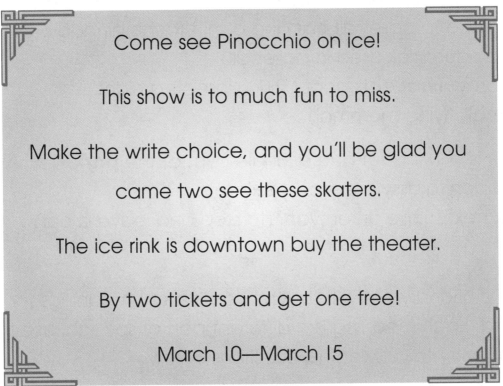

Come see Pinocchio on ice!

This show is to much fun to miss.

Make the write choice, and you'll be glad you

came two see these skaters.

The ice rink is downtown buy the theater.

By two tickets and get one free!

March 10—March 15

Try It

1. Write a sentence using the word **too**.

   _____

2. Write a sentence using the word **buy**.

   _____

3. Write a sentence using the word **write**.

   _____

Lesson 3.21 Multiple-Meaning Words

Multiple-meaning words are words that are spelled the same but have different meanings. You have to read the sentence carefully to know which meaning a writer wants to use.

Casey got a baseball **bat** and a mitt for his birthday.
(a wooden stick used in baseball)
The brown **bat** eats about 2,000 insects a night.
(a small, flying mammal)

There is a swing set and a jungle gym at the **park**.
(an open, grassy area for relaxing)
Park next to the green van. (to stop and leave a car)

Find It

Read this dictionary entry. It shows two different meanings for the same word. Each meaning is a different part of speech. Use the dictionary entry to answer the questions below.

cold *adj.* having a low temperature; cool, chilly, or icy; not warm; *noun* an illness that often includes a cough, a sore throat, and a runny nose

1. It will be cold but sunny on Saturday.

   Which definition of **cold** is used in this sentence? _____
   a. the first definition   **b.** the second definition

2. Destiny caught a cold from her brother.
   Which definition of **cold** is used in this sentence? _____
   a. the first definition   **b.** the second definition

Lesson 3.21 Multiple-Meaning Words

Match It

Look at the definitions of the underlined word. Choose the definition that matches the way the word is used. Write the letter of that definition on the line.

1. _____ Airplanes <u>fly</u> at amazing speeds.
   a. a small insect with two wings
   b. to move through the air

2. _____ The <u>leaves</u> were red, gold, and brown.
   a. parts of a tree or a plant   **b.** goes away

3. _____ May I <u>pet</u> your cat?
   a. an animal that lives with people
   b. to touch lightly or stroke

4. _____ The Krugers did not <u>watch</u> the entire movie.
   a. view or look at   **b.** a small clock worn on the wrist

5. _____ Keely will <u>train</u> her puppy to roll over.
   a. to teach something by doing it over and over
   b. a long line of cars that run on a track

Try It

The word **fair** can have two meanings: **equal** or **a place, like a carnival, where there are rides and games**. Write two sentences using the word **fair**. It should have a different meaning in each sentence.

1. _____

2. _____

Before you start writing, you need to make a plan. **Brainstorming** is one way to come up with ideas. You may not use all of your ideas. Still, you will find the one or two great ideas you were looking for.

Sit down with a pen and a piece of paper. Make a list of things you know a lot about or would like to learn more about.

life in the Sahara desert	Eiffel Tower
basketball	space shuttles
islands	being an artist

Which topic is most interesting? Once you choose your topic, you can start learning more about it. You may need to go to the library. You may need to use the Internet. You may even need to interview someone.

Once you have all your information, make an **idea web**. It can help you put your ideas in order before you start writing.

popular landmark

world's fair

people against it

Eiffel Tower

tallest building

Paris, France

Try It

On a separate piece of paper, brainstorm your own list of ideas. Let your imagination go, and have fun! Choose the most interesting topic. If you need to, look for more information. Then, create an idea web.

Lesson 4.2 Writer's Guide: Writing

When you first begin writing, do not worry about mistakes. You are just writing a **rough draft**. Look at the idea web you made when you were planning. Turn your ideas into sentences and paragraphs.

Do not worry about editing right now. After you have written your first draft, you can make changes and corrections. For now, just write. Here are some things to keep in mind as you write:

- Stay on topic.
- Include all the important details.
- Use complete sentences.

Here is an example of a rough draft. Can you see how the writer used the idea web to help write this paragraph?

The Eiffel Tower is an intresting place to visit. It was built in Paris France. It was made for a world's fair The Louvre is a famous museum in Paris. The tower is very tall. It was the tallest building in the world many people did not think it should be built. it looks like they were wrong, though. Millions of people visit it every year! It is one of the most famus landmarks.

Try It

Use the idea web you made to write a rough draft on another piece of paper. Remember, this stage is all about writing, so write! You'll be able to edit your work later.

Lesson 4.3 Writer's Guide: Revising

Now that you have finished writing, it is time to **revise**. Read what you have written. Sometimes it helps to read your work out loud. Ask yourself these questions:

- Do all of my sentences tell about the main idea?
- Can I add any details that make my writing more interesting?
- Are there any words or sentences that do not belong?

The Eiffel tower is an intresting place to visit. It was built in *in 1889*

Paris France. It was made for a world's fair. ~~The Louvre is a famous~~

~~museum in Paris.~~ The tower is *986 feet* very tall. It was the tallest building in

for 41 years the world many people did not think it should be built. *They thought it would be ugly.* it looks like

they were wrong, though. *About 6* Millions of people visit *The Eiffel tower* it every year! It is

in the world one of the most famus landmarks.

In the paragraph above, the writer added some details. For example, explaining that the Eiffel Tower is very tall does not tell the reader much. It is more helpful to know that the Eiffel Tower is 986 feet tall.

The writer also took out a sentence that was not needed. The Louvre is in Paris, but it does not have anything to do with the Eiffel Tower. The writer decided that the sentence about the Louvre was not on topic.

Try It

Look at all the changes the writer made. Can you see why each change was needed? Now, revise your rough draft. Doesn't it sound better already?

Lesson 4.4 Writer's Guide: Proofreading

Proofreading makes your writing stronger and clearer. Here are some things to ask yourself when you are proofreading:

- Do sentences and proper nouns start with a capital letter?
- Does each sentence end with a punctuation mark?
- Are any words misspelled? Use a dictionary if you are not sure.
- Are commas used in the right places?

	Proofreading Marks	
∧	= add, or insert	The cat sat in the window. (black inserted)
∧,	= add a comma	the tiny spotted mushroom
g̲ (G)	= capitalize	meg (M)
⊙	= add a period	We picked the tomatoes⊙
⫫	= lowercase	The Painting is on the wall.

    The Eiffel Tower is an intresting (e) place to visit. It was built in 1889

in Paris France. It was made for a world's fair. The tower is 986 feet

tall. It was the tallest building in the world for 41 years many people (M)

did not think it should be built. They thought it would be ugly. it looks

like they were wrong, though. About six Million people visit the Eiffel

tower every year! It is one of the most famus landmarks in the world.

Try It

Use proofreading marks to edit your writing. Trade papers with a friend. It can be easier to spot mistakes in someone else's work.

Lesson 4.5 Writer's Guide: Publishing

After all your changes have been made, write or type a final copy of your work. Your paper should look neat and clean. Now, you are ready to publish. **Publishing** is a way of sharing your writing with others. Here are some ways to publish your work:

- Read your writing to your family, your friends, or your classmates.
- Make a copy of your writing. Send it to someone who lives far away.
- Read your writing aloud. Have a teacher or parent record you. You can use a video camera or a tape recorder.
- Make copies, and give them to your friends.
- Ask an adult to help you e-mail your writing to a friend or a family member.
- Get together with some other students. Make copies of everyone's writing. Combine the copies into a booklet that each student can take home.

From: Tucker Boone
Date: May 20, 2015
To: auntlouisa@smileyhorse.net; grandpajoe@21stcentury.com
Subject: Eiffel Tower report

   The Eiffel Tower is an interesting place to visit. It was built in 1889 in Paris, France. It was made for a world's fair. The tower is 986 feet tall. It was the tallest building in the world for 41 years. Many people did not think it should be built. They thought it would be ugly. It looks like they were wrong, though. About six million people visit the Eiffel Tower every year! It is one of the most famous landmarks in the world.

Try It

Choose one of the ways listed above to share your work. What kinds of comments do your friends and family have? Can you think of any other ways to share your writing?

Lesson 4.6 Writer's Guide: Writing a Paragraph

A **paragraph** is a group of sentences. Each paragraph is about one main idea. All the sentences tell more about the main idea. When you are ready to write about a new idea, start a new paragraph. When the paragraphs are put together, they make a letter, a story, or a report.

A new paragraph does not start at the left edge of a piece of paper. It starts about five spaces from the edge. Leave an **indent**, or a space, about the size of the word **write**. This space tells the reader a new paragraph is starting.

The first sentence in a paragraph is the **topic sentence**. It tells what the paragraph will be mostly about. The next few sentences give more details about the topic. The last sentence is a **closing sentence**. It sums up the paragraph.

In the paragraph below, each important part is labeled.

indent   topic sentence

details

→ The Eiffel Tower is an interesting place to visit. It was built in 1889 in Paris, France. It was made for a world's fair. The tower is 986 feet tall. It was the tallest building in the world for 41 years. Many people did not think it should be built. They thought it would be ugly. It looks like they were wrong, though. About six million people visit the Eiffel Tower every year! It is one of the most famous landmarks in the world.

closing sentence

Lesson 4.7 Writer's Guide: Writing a Friendly Letter

Writing a letter can be fun. It is exciting to open the mailbox and see a letter waiting. Writing letters can also be a good way to keep in touch with people who live far away.

Here are some things to keep in mind when you write a letter:

- **Write the date in the top right corner.** Remember to start the name of the month with a capital letter. Use a comma between the day and the year.
- **Begin your letter with a greeting.** Follow it with the person's name and a comma. Most letters begin with the word **Dear**.
- **Share some news in your letter.** What is new in your life? Have you done anything fun? Have you been someplace exciting?
- **Ask questions.** It is polite to ask how others are doing.
- **End your letter with a closing.** Some popular closings are **Sincerely**, **Yours truly**, **Love**, and **Your friend**. Use a capital letter to begin your closing. Use a comma after it.
- **Sign your name** below the closing.

May 20, 2014

Dear Grandma,

How are you? I am doing fine. Last week, I wrote a report about the Eiffel Tower. Mom helped me do some research on the Internet. I learned many interesting facts. For example, did you know that the Eiffel Tower has 1,665 steps? Mr. Strasser said my report was excellent. I told him that I plan to see the Eiffel Tower in person someday.

Please write back to me, and tell me what's new in Park City. I miss you a lot and hope you can visit soon.

Love,

Tucker

Lesson 4.8 Writer's Guide: Writing to Convince

Have you ever tried to convince someone of something? To **convince** means **to get people to see things your way**. Maybe you have tried to convince your teacher that recess should be longer. Maybe you have tried to convince your parents to give you a later bedtime.

Words can be very powerful. You can change people's ideas with your words. Here are some tips for writing to convince:

- Think of all the reasons you feel a certain way. Make a list of your ideas.
- Now, think about why people might not agree with you. What could you say to change their minds? Add these ideas to your list.
- You are ready to begin writing. First, write a topic sentence about what you want or believe. Next, list your reasons. Finally, write a sentence that sums up your ideas.

Eiffel Tower should be free	**it's a public place**
	more people might visit if free
	people could donate money
	money used to care for tower

People should not have to pay to visit the Eiffel Tower. The tower is like a park or a library. It belongs to everyone. People should be able to enjoy it at any time. Instead of paying to see it, people could donate money if they wanted. This money could be used to take care of the tower. More people might visit the Eiffel Tower if they did not have to pay. It should be free for everyone to enjoy.

SPECTRUM®

Reading

Dad's First Day

Read to see why Dad is upset.

1 I think Dad is nervous. At breakfast, he almost poured milk into his orange juice instead of into his cereal bowl! Mom doesn't seem worried. She knows why Dad is a little upset. Today is his first day at a new job.

2 My dad builds bridges. Some of them look heavy and strong. Others look light, as if they are just hanging in the air. Dad says the light bridges are just as strong as the heavy ones.

3 Dad is an excellent bridge builder, even at home. Once, we almost filled my whole room with bridges. We used boxes, blocks, pots, pans, and even the dog's dish. It was great.

4 I know Dad has tons of great bridge ideas, so he shouldn't be nervous. I guess he just wants to practice making one more bridge before he goes to work.

1. What kinds of bridges does Dad build?

_____

2. Why is Dad nervous?

_____

3. How does the boy know that Dad is nervous?

_____

4. What kind of bridge did the boy and Dad make at home?

_____

_____

5. From whose point of view is the story told?

_____

6. The last line of the story says that Dad is going to make one more bridge at home. What does he use to make it?

_____

_____

_____

7. Is the first sentence of the story a fact or an opinion?

_____

Bridges

What kinds of bridges are there?

1   Have you ever stepped on a stone to get across a puddle or stream? If you have, you were using a bridge.

2   Bridges are different sizes and shapes. Some bridges have straight "legs," or supports, called beams. Other bridges have curved supports, called arches. Still others actually hang from strong steel ropes, or cables, that are strung above the surface of the bridge. The cables are then attached to the land on either end of the bridge.

3   Most bridges go over water, but some bridges were made to carry water. About 2,000 years ago, the Romans built this kind of bridge. One such bridge, in France, had three levels. Water flowed in the top level, and people and carts traveled on the two lower levels.

1. This passage is mostly about

_____ old bridges.

_____ kinds of bridges.

_____ making bridges.

2. The author wrote this selection to

_____ make you laugh.   _____ help you learn.

3. Think about what you already know about bridges. What are bridges for?

_____

4. This passage tells about another use for bridges. What is it?

_____

5. Are all bridges made by humans? What might a natural bridge be made of?

_____

_____

6. How are bridges with arches and beams different?

_____

_____

7. *The Golden Gate Bridge is the prettiest bridge in the U.S.* Is this a fact or an opinion?

_____

Bridges to Remember

Read to find out what is special about these bridges.

1   Some people do not like to drive across bridges. They look straight ahead and try to hold their breath until they get to the other side. Good luck if those people are driving in Louisiana. There is a 24-mile-long bridge there! It takes about half an hour to get across.

2   If you like to look way, way down when you cross a bridge, you should go to Colorado. A bridge there stands more than a thousand feet above a river. A 75-story building could fit under that bridge!

3   If you do not like to look down, get in the middle lane of a bridge in Australia. It has eight lanes for cars, two train tracks, a bike path, and a sidewalk.

4   Finally, if you like crowds and bridges, go to India. A bridge there carries 100,000 cars and trucks every day, plus thousands of walkers.

1. How does the text help you understand how long a 24-mile-long bridge is?

_____

2. How does the text help you understand how high the bridge in Colorado is?

_____

_____

3. If you do not like to look over the side of a bridge, why would the bridge in Australia be a good one to cross?

_____

4. Why is the bridge in India a bridge to remember?

_____

_____

5. Name three things, other than cars, that cross bridges in the selection.

_____

_____

_____

6. What do some people do if they are nervous on a bridge?

_____

_____

Moving Out Day

Read to see how Emily feels about moving.

1 *There goes another box,* thought Emily. *All my stuff is in boxes. It's all getting squashed together.*

2 Mom stood on the front steps. "Oh, be careful with that one!" she cried. The movers nodded as they went past. *All my stuff is in boxes,* thought Mom. *It might all get broken.*

3 Dad came out of the garage. "Wow, this is a heavy one! It might break everything else." Mom and Emily frowned.

4 An hour later, the boxes were still going past. One box had holes in it. Emily had made the holes so her stuffed animals could get some air.

5 Finally, they all watched the movers close up the truck. *Ka-thunk* went the big doors. Dad gave Emily a little hug. "One empty house and one full truck. That's a good day's work."

1. What do Mom and Emily worry about?

_____

2. Circle the word that best tells how Emily feels about her stuffed animals.

hopeless   caring   harsh

3. What word best tells how Mom feels? Circle it.

relaxed   worried   careless

4. How do you think Dad feels about moving day?

_____

5. What clues in the story help you know how Dad feels?

_____

6. How do you think Emily will feel when the move is complete? Explain.

_____

_____

7. Why did Emily put holes in one of the boxes?

_____

8. How does the picture on page 196 add to your understanding of the story?

_____

_____

Moving In Day

What does Emily think of her new home?

1 "Emily, would you go turn on the lights, please?" asked Mom. "The movers will need to see when they bring our stuff in."

2 "Sure, Mom." Emily was happy to check out the new house. She turned on twelve lights and then went back to Mom.

3 "Why don't you help me unpack this box?" asked Mom.

4 "Sure, Mom," said Emily.

5 Mom and Emily lifted out shapes wrapped in newspaper. One was the cookie jar. Another was a mug. Then, Mom unwrapped a roll of paper.

6 "Oh, look, Emily! It's the picture you drew last summer!" Emily saw the picture she had made of her family. They were all smiling. The picture made Emily smile, even here in the new house.

7 Mom smiled, too. "Let's put it on the refrigerator," they said together. And they did.

1. Why was Emily happy to go turn on the lights?

_____

2. How did the picture make Emily feel?

_____

_____

3. How did Emily feel about her new house?

_____

_____

4. Write **1**, **2**, and **3** by these sentences to show what happened first, next, and last.

_____ Emily turned on the lights.

_____ Mom and Emily put a picture on the refrigerator.

_____ Mom and Emily unpacked a box.

5. How would you feel about moving to a new home? Why?

_____

_____

6. Do you think Emily's mom understands how Emily feels? Explain.

_____

_____

_____

Boxes, Books, and More

How do Emily's feelings about the new house change?

1 Emily pushed a box across the floor. Her room was so empty! She didn't like it. Her old room had been pink. This one was just plain white.

2 Emily's mom poked her head in. "Do you need any help?"

3 "No, I'm okay, Mom. I'm going to unpack my books first."

4 "That sounds good," said Mom. "I'll just make up your bed. Okay?"

5 "Thanks, Mom." Emily put the biggest books on the bottom shelf. She put the medium books on the middle shelf. She put the smallest books on the top shelf. It took a long time because she stopped to read some of them along the way.

6 Emily stepped back. All of her books were in place. Her quilt was on her bed. Everything looked just right.

1. This story is mostly about

_____ Emily's new room.

_____ how busy Mom is.

_____ Emily's toys.

2. At the beginning of the story, what does Emily think about her new room?

_____

3. What does Emily think of her room at the end of the story?

_____

4. What happened to change Emily's feelings?

_____

_____

5. How does Emily organize her books?

_____

6. How does Mom help Emily with her room?

_____

7. What do you think Emily will do next in the story? Make a check mark next to your answer.

_____ Go on a bike ride

_____ Unpack more things in her room

_____ Call her grandma

No Boxes Today

Read to see what Emily learns about her new home.

1 "Who is tired of unpacking boxes?" asked Dad at breakfast. Mom and Emily laughed and raised their hands high.

2 "Why don't we go on a little tour? We won't even think about boxes today," said Dad.

3 "What will we tour, Dad?" asked Emily.

4 "We'll tour our new city. San Antonio is an exciting place."

5 "Are there old houses?" asked Emily. She liked old houses.

6 "Yes, there are, but I thought we might start at the Children's Museum."

7 Emily grinned. "There is a museum just for me? Wow!"

8 "And after that," said Dad, "we can ride in a river taxi."

9 "Okay, let's go!" said Emily, jumping up from the table.

10 Mom and Dad laughed. "Maybe you should get dressed first, Emily."

Look at each picture and circle the sentence that goes with it.

1. Emily is eating breakfast.

Emily is making her bed.

2. Dad is carrying a box.

Dad is unpacking a box.

3. What meal is the family eating?

_____

4. Why can't the family leave right away?

_____

5. What is the setting for this story?

_____

6. Read each sentence. If it is a fact, write **F** on the line. If it is an opinion, write **O**.

_____ San Antonio is an exciting place.

_____ Mom and Emily laughed and raised their hands high.

_____ We can ride in a river taxi.

The Texas Story

What do you know about Texas? Read to see what else you can learn.

How Big Is Texas?

1   Texas is the second-largest state in the United States. Only Alaska is larger. Texas is also second when it comes to the number of people living in the state. Only California has more people than Texas.

How Old Is Texas?

2   On December 29, 1845, Texas became a state. It was the twenty-eighth state. In 2015, Texas is turning 170 years old.

What Comes From Texas?

3   The huge state of Texas gives us many things to eat and use. Many farmers raise cattle for beef and milk. Other farmers grow grapefruit, which is Texas's state fruit.

4   There is much oil in Texas. Once oil is drilled out of the ground, it is used to make many things, including gas for our cars and plastic.

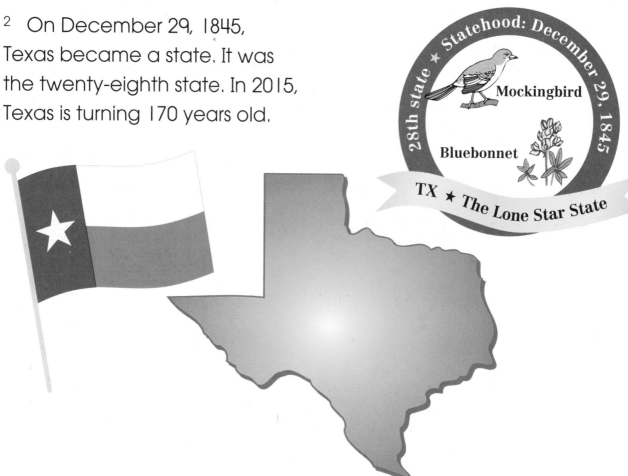

Statehood: December 29, 1845 ★ 28th state

Mockingbird

Bluebonnet

TX ★ The Lone Star State

1. What did you already know about Texas?

_____

2. List two new things you learned about Texas.

_____

_____

3. What question would you like to ask about Texas?

_____

_____

4. Why do you think the author wrote this article about Texas?

_____ to help the reader learn something

_____ to make the reader laugh

5. How do the boldface headings help organize the text?

_____

_____

6. What are two things you learned from the illustrations that are not in the text?

_____

_____

7. Complete the sentence: Texas is number two both in

_____ and _____ .

San Antonio Today

Do you think you would like to visit San Antonio?

1 In San Antonio today, a visitor can learn many things about Texas's past. Many old buildings still stand. At the same time, it is a modern city. People visit San Antonio to eat, shop, go to concerts, and see the sights. The city's River Walk is a common place to go. The San Antonio River flows right through downtown. Along the river are many shops and hotels. Beautiful plants grow along the River Walk, too. Many bridges and stairways help people get from one place to another.

2 If you don't feel like walking, you might choose to ride a streetcar. You can see all of downtown and the River Walk from your seat. Or, if you like the water, you can take a river taxi. River taxis travel all along the 21 blocks of the River Walk.

NAME _____

Write each word in the correct blank.

city	hotels	concert	ride

1. If you like music, go to a _____.

2. San Antonio is a large, modern _____.

3. If you are tired, _____ in a river taxi.

4. People sleep in _____ along the River Walk.

5. Which word best describes the city of San Antonio?

_____ rundown

_____ beautiful

_____ cold

6. If you visited San Antonio, what would you most like to do?

_____

_____

7. What do you think a river taxi is?

_____

_____

Paul Bunyan: A New Story

Read this tall tale to find out how Paul Bunyan solves a problem.

1   After the great race, everyone in Minnesota was wondering what to do about all the holes. The giant lumberjack Paul Bunyan and his big blue ox, Babe, had made the holes with their feet. People couldn't plow their fields or walk through the woods any more. Every time they tried, they fell into one of those holes. Paul felt terrible, but Babe felt so badly that he ran away. Paul climbed the Black Hills to see if he could spot his blue ox. Then, he looked under the Mississippi River, but Babe wasn't there.

2   At the end of the day, Paul just sat down and cried. He cried so hard that all of those holes filled up with water. The people in Minnesota got out their boats and fishing poles. They thanked Paul so loudly that Babe heard them and came home to Paul.

1. How did Paul solve the problem with the holes?

_____

_____

2. Why did Babe run away?

_____

_____

3. What made Babe come back?

_____

4. People who tell tall tales stretch the truth. List one idea from the story that can't be true.

_____

_____

5. What is the story's setting? _____

6. Why did the people of Minnesota thank Paul?

_____

_____

7. What causes Paul Bunyan to cry?

_____

8. Who is the main character in the story?

_____

Afternoon Art

Read to see what Mom and Matt draw.

1 "May I have the green, please?" asked Matt.

2 "Sure," said Mom. She handed it over. "Are you making more trees?"

3 "No," said Matt, "I'm done with trees. I'm drawing a turtle now. What are you working on?"

4 Mom held up her paper. A big orange flower filled the page. Matt smiled. "That's the flower in Gram's garden, isn't it?"

5 "That's what I'm trying to make it look like," said Mom. "Drawing pretty flowers helps me remember them when the flowers are all gone."

6 Matt nodded. "And drawing this turtle helps me remember the one we saw by the road last week."

7 "May I have the orange, please?" asked Mom.

8 "More flowers?" Matt asked.

9 "No. Cheese," teased Mom. "I'm trying to remember my lunch. I'm hungry."

NAME _____

1. This story is mostly about

_____ how to draw.

_____ Matt and Mom drawing.

_____ choosing colors.

Circle the best answer.

2. What do you think Mom and Matt will do next?

get ready for bed   go to school   have a snack

3. Write **1**, **2**, and **3** in the spaces below to show in what order events happened.

_____ Mom shows Matt her flower.

_____ Mom says she is hungry.

_____ Matt says he is drawing a turtle.

4. There is a lot of dialogue in the story. Write one example of dialogue on the line. Tell how you know that it is dialogue.

_____

_____

5. At the end of the story, do you think Mom will really draw cheese? Why or why not?

_____

6. What does drawing a turtle make Matt think of?

_____

What Is an Art Museum?

Read to find out what an art museum is.

1   Art comes in all sizes and shapes. It might be pretty, or it might be unusual. If you look for it, you can see art all around you. It might be a building, a picture on a poster, or a shape in the sand.

2   A place where people display art so that other people can see it is called an *art museum*. Some museums take care of art that is very old. Old art helps us learn about the people who made it long, long ago.

3   Some museums display new art. New art helps us see the world in different ways. It might make us ask questions, or it might make us laugh.

4   Most big cities have art museums. Some are big and famous. Others are small and not well known. All of them take good care of their art, though, so that people can see it and learn about it.

1. What is the author's purpose in writing this piece?

_____ to entertain

_____ to teach

_____ to persuade

2. What can we learn from new art?

_____

3. What can we learn from old art?

_____

_____

4. Tell in your own words what an art museum is.

_____

5. Name two ways that art museums can be different from each other.

_____

_____

6. In the first paragraph, the text says that you can see art all around you. What art can you see right now?

_____

7. If you visited an art museum, what kind of art would you hope to see?

_____

Animal Shelter News

What is Carly excited about?

1   Carly's fork dropped against her plate. She felt her face turn red. Her dad had invited a friend from work for dinner. Mr. Mendez was right next to Carly. She felt a little nervous.

2   "Mrs. Blake," said Mr. Mendez, "thank you for such a fine meal. I do wish my wife had been able to come."

3   "You're welcome, and so do we," Mrs. Blake smiled. "Did you say there was a problem at work?"

4   "Yes," said Mr. Mendez, nodding his head. "She has been working extra hours. The animal shelter is so busy in spring."

5   "Why is it so busy?" Carly asked.

6   Mr. Mendez looked down at Carly. "This is the time of year when many kittens are born."

7   "Kittens!" said Carly so loudly that her face turned red again. "Did you hear that, Mom?"

1. Why does Carly's face turn red the first time?

_____

2. Why couldn't Mrs. Mendez come to dinner?

_____

3. Based on your reading of the story, where do you think Mrs. Mendez works?

_____

4. Why does Carly's face turn red the second time?

_____

Circle the best answer.

5. What do you think will happen next?

Mrs. Mendez will arrive.   Carly will ask for a kitten.

Carly's cat will enter the room.

6. Write **T** for *true* or **F** for *false* next to each sentence below.

_____ Carly's dad works with Mr. Mendez.

_____ Carly's family has three cats.

_____ When Carly is embarrassed, her face turns red.

_____ The animal shelter is busy in the spring.

7. Why is the animal shelter extra busy in spring?

_____

The Case for a Cat

What does Carly's family talk about after dinner?

1 "Did you hear what Mr. Mendez said about the animal shelter?" Carly asked. "They have *too many kittens!*"

2 Mom was washing dishes. She didn't turn around. "Yes, it's sad that so many animals don't have homes."

3 "We could give one a home!" said Carly. Now, Mom turned around, shaking her head.

4 "Dad and I would like you to have a pet," explained Mom, "but our apartment is so small."

5 "The Hamlins live just two apartments down. They have a cat," objected Carly.

6 Mom frowned. She looked at Dad. "Dad and I will have to talk about it," she said slowly. "We need to think hard about whether we are ready for a cat or not."

7 "Okay," said Carly. Then, she grinned. "If you need any help, let me know. I'll help you think."

1. This story is mostly about

_____ cats and dogs as pets.

_____ a girl who wants a kitten.

_____ doing chores at home.

2. Carly thinks getting a cat is a good idea. What reasons does she give?

_____

3. What reason does Mom give for not getting a pet?

_____

4. What would you do if you were Carly?

_____

5. Look at the last line of the first paragraph. The words *too many kittens* are in italics. Why do you think the author used italics here?

_____

6. In paragraph 5, Carly *objects* to what her mom says. What does it mean to object?

_____

7. At the end of the story, why does Carly offer to help her parents think about getting a cat?

_____

_____

Cats Long Ago

Read to learn part of the history of cats.

1   Imagine that it is three thousand years ago. You are visiting Egypt. You see a statue of a cat. You go into a building, and there are cats everywhere! People are feeding them and taking care of them. Everyone seems to like cats.

2   "Why so many cats?" you wonder. To answer that question, we have to learn a little bit about Egypt.

3   The Egyptians grew grain for food and to trade with other people. They stored their grain in huge buildings. Rats and mice, in particular, also liked to eat grain. Cats, which eat rats and mice, were the best way to protect the grain.

4   Cats became the most respected animal in Egypt. When a family's cat died, the family members shaved their eyebrows to show that a sad and important thing had happened.

1. The author wrote "Cats Long Ago" mostly to

_____ give information.

_____ make you laugh.

2. Compare what you know about cats in Egypt with what you know about cats today. One idea is written for you.

In Egypt <u>cats were respected</u> _____

_____

Today <u>cats are usually well cared for</u> _____

_____

3. What is one difference between us and the people in Egypt long ago?

_____

4. What did Egyptians do when a family cat died?

_____

5. How were cats helpful to Egyptians long ago?

_____

Use the text to fill in the blank in each sentence below.

6. Rats and mice ate the _____ that Egyptians stored.

7. Cats were the most _____ animals in Egypt.

8. Cats helped to _____ the grain.

Cats Every Day

What kind of care does a cat need?

1 Like all house pets, cats need food, water, and a certain amount of attention every day.

Food

2 A cat needs its food dish filled every day. A box of cat food costs several dollars. An adult cat may eat a box in less than two weeks.

Water

3 A cat needs to have fresh water each day. You will probably have to fill the dish twice a day.

Other Needs

4 If a cat lives indoors, it needs a litter box. Cat litter costs several dollars for a 10-pound bag. The bag lasts for several weeks. The litter box, however, should be cleaned out almost every day.

5 Once a cat becomes your pet, it will depend on you for almost all of its needs. Are you ready?

1. This article is mostly about

_____ cats in animal shelters.

_____ how cute kittens are.

_____ daily cat care.

2. After reading the article, do you think you could care for a cat? Why or why not?

_____

3. Write one idea that you find under each heading.

Food _____

Water _____

Other Needs _____

4. Why do you think the author used headings in this article?

_____

5. Read each sentence. Write **F** if it is a fact and **O** if it is an opinion.

_____ A cat needs to be fed every day.

_____ Cats make the best pets!

_____ If you have an indoor cat, it needs a litter box.

_____ If you adopt a cat, you should choose an older cat.

6. How often does a litter box need to be cleaned?

_____

Comb the Cat, Please!

What does a cat need besides food and water?

Grooming

1   Cats are very clean animals. They use their rough tongues to bathe themselves several times a day. Sometimes they like help, though. To keep a cat's coat in shape, it is a good idea to comb or brush the cat once or twice a week. If you have a long-haired cat, you may need to brush it every day to keep its fur neat.

Health Care

2   All kittens should visit a vet and get several shots. These shots help prevent common cat illnesses. An adult cat should visit a vet once a year for a check-up and to get booster shots.

3   Unless your family plans to breed and raise cats, your cat should have an operation so that it cannot have kittens. This prevents unwanted kittens from ending up stray or at the animal shelter.

1. What do cats do for themselves?

_____

2. What should a cat owner do once a year?

_____

3. Why might a long-haired cat need to be brushed more often than a short-haired cat?

_____

_____

4. If you had a cat, would you rather have a short-haired cat or a long-haired cat? Write why.

_____

_____

5. Why do cats need to have an operation?

_____

6. The text says that cats have rough tongues. How do you think this is helpful when they groom themselves?

_____

_____

7. Is it important to be a responsible cat owner? Explain.

_____

_____

Cat or No Cat?

Will Carly get the kitten she wants?

1 "Carly, would you and Mitch come here, please? We want to talk to you about something," Dad called from the kitchen.

2 "Coming, Dad," said Carly. To her little brother, she said, "Come on, Mitch. Maybe this is about a kitten!"

3 Mom and Dad were sitting at the kitchen table. They looked thoughtful. Carly and Mitch sat down. Dad spoke first. Carly's heart sank. Dad always gave out the bad news. "Your mother and I have been talking about a cat." Carly held on to a tiny bit of hope.

4 Then, Mom began to speak. Carly perked up a little. "We don't think a kitten is a good idea." *Boom!* Carly's spirits sank again.

5 Mom went on, "We think it would be better if we got a grown-up cat."

1. At the beginning of the story, what did you predict would happen at the end?

_____

2. Why does Carly worry when Dad speaks first?

_____

3. Have you ever wanted something as much as Carly wants a kitten? Tell about it.

_____

4. In the story, who is Mitch?

_____ Carly's dad _____ Carly's brother _____ Carly's cousin

5. Why do you think Carly's parents want an older cat and not a kitten?

_____

6. Do you think Carly will be happy about her parents' decision? Why or why not?

_____

7. Look at the picture on page 224. What does the art add to the story? How do the kids looks like they are feeling?

_____

8. Read the last line of the story again. What do you predict will happen next?

_____

Choose a Cat

Which cat will Carly and Mitch choose?

1 "It's our first pet, so we would like to start with a grown-up cat," explained Mom.

2 Mrs. Mendez smiled. "I think that's a smart idea for a first pet. It's a little easier. Feel free to look around. Just wave if you have questions," said Mrs. Mendez as she turned away.

3 Carly and Mitch were already looking around. An orange tiger cat looked at Mitch, but then it walked away. Carly saw a big black cat. She held out her hand. The cat hissed and batted at her hand.

4 "You are not very friendly!" cried Carly, pulling her hand back. Just then, a gray cat with white paws rubbed against Carly's ankles, then against Mitch's.

5 Mitch smiled at Carly. "This one has picked us, Carly."

1. This story is mostly about

_____ choosing a cat.

_____ Mr. Mendez's work.

_____ kittens who need homes.

2. Why didn't Carly choose the big black cat?

_____

3. How did Mitch and Carly choose the gray cat?

_____

4. What does it mean when a cat hisses at you?

_____

5. Mrs. Mendez comes up in an earlier story. How does Carly's family know her?

_____

6. Why does Mrs. Mendez think a grown up cat is a good choice for a first pet?

_____

7. What is the setting for this story?

_____

8. Do you think the Blake family will be good pet owners? Why or why not?

_____

Mouse in the House

Read about Mouse's first day in his new home.

1 Carly opened her eyes and stretched. What was special about today?

2 "Oh," she cried, throwing back the covers. "Mouse! Where are you? Here, kitty, kitty, kitty!"

3 It had been easy to pick a name for the new cat. He was gray, and he made a tiny little mewing sound. "Mouse" was perfect. But where was he now? Carly looked under her bed. Mitch looked, too.

4 Carly passed through the kitchen. "Mom, have you seen Mouse?"

5 "Not since I gave him his breakfast," she said over the newspaper. "Did you try the living room?"

6 On the living room floor was a big patch of sunshine. Right in the middle was Mouse. He was curled up and sound asleep.

7 Mouse was at home.

1. Which sentence best tells how Carly feels about today?

_____ She is excited.

_____ She is worried.

2. What words or ideas in the story helped you answer question **1**?

_____

_____

3. Where did Carly and Mitch look first for Mouse?

_____

4. In what room did Carly find Mouse?

_____

5. Why was Mouse sleeping there?

_____

6. Why do Carly and Mitch name their cat Mouse?

_____

_____

7. Why is the title of the story funny?

_____

_____

8. How do you think Carly feels about her new cat?

_____

A Letter from Kyle

What news does Kyle send to his grandparents?

Dear Grandma and Grandpa,

1 How are you? I am fine. School is out already. On our last day, we had a picnic out on the baseball field. It was fun until we all had to dash out of the rain. Even that was kind of fun, though.

2 How was your camping trip? Dad says you're just getting back home today. We took good care of Sparky for you. He sleeps at the foot of my bed on most nights. He and the cat have even been getting along. I think Snowy must have had a talk with Sparky. When Snowy walks into the room, Sparky leaves!

3 Dad says to tell you that our garden is looking good this year. We've had lots of rain, especially on that last day of school.

4 When are you coming to get Sparky? See you soon.

Love,
Kyle

1. Why was there a picnic on the baseball field?

_____

2. Why did everyone have to dash into the school?

_____

3. Why is Kyle's family taking care of Sparky?

_____

4. Why does Sparky leave the room when Snowy comes in?

_____

5. What kind of animal is Sparky? How do you know?

_____

_____

6. Think of what you learned about Kyle by reading his letter. Write three words you could use to describe him.

_____   _____   _____

7. In what time of year does the story take place?

_____ winter   _____ fall   _____ summer

8. What clues in the text helped you answer number 7?

_____

_____

Kyle Gets Mail

What did Kyle's grandparents see on their camping trip?

Dear Kyle,

1 Our camping trip was wonderful! We're already talking about going to the same place next year. There is so much to see. I think you and your parents would like it, too.

2 From Ohio, we drove south to Kentucky. We enjoy looking at rocks, so we had decided to go to Mammoth Cave State Park. We made the right choice! I've never seen so many rocks!

3 Each day, we chose a different cave. We saw narrow places and huge, high rooms. In one cave, we were underground for more than two miles.

4 We'll come to get Sparky next weekend, if that's okay. We hope he hasn't been unhappy.

Love,
Grandma and Grandpa

1. Where did Kyle's grandparents go on their trip?

_____

2. Why did they go there?

_____

3. What did you learn about Kyle's grandparents by reading their letter?

_____

_____

4. Where do Grandma and Grandpa live? _____

5. Read each sentence. Write **F** if it is a fact and **O** if it is an opinion.

_____ You and your parents would like it, too.

_____ Our camping trip was wonderful!

_____ We were underground for more than two miles.

_____ Each day, we chose a different cave.

6. Based on their letter, you know that Grandma and Grandpa probably

_____ live in Kentucky.

_____ like to have adventures.

_____ have several dogs.

7. What is the purpose of Grandma and Grandpa's letter?

_____

Mammoth Cave, Kentucky

What would you like to see at Mammoth Cave?

1 For natural beauty, there is no spot quite like Mammoth Cave National Park. Beneath the park lies the longest cave system on Earth. There are more than 350 miles of underground passages. That's more than three times longer than any other cave we know about. Some scientists think that there are hundreds of miles yet to be found!

2 If you go, you can follow a path that humans walked on four thousand years ago. You can see crystals that are millions of years old. If you're lucky, you might see an eyeless fish.

3 Though the cave passages are dark, more than 200 kinds of animals live in them. Many of these use the cave only part of the time. Some, however, can live only in the dark, cool cave.

1. This article is mostly about

_____ how caves are formed.

_____ the sights in Mammoth Cave.

_____ animals that live in caves.

2. What is special about Mammoth Cave?

_____

3. Why might a fish that lives in a cave not have any eyes?

_____

4. If you went to Mammoth Cave, what would you most like to see? Write why.

_____

5. Name two types of animals that are likely to live in Mammoth Cave.

_____   _____

6. Based on the article, how do you think the author feels about Mammoth Cave?

_____

7. How long do you think humans have known about the cave?

_____

8. Why are the caves still a mystery to scientists?

_____

Post by Post

What is hard about painting a fence?

1 "Is this everything we need, Dad?" Michelle looked at her dad in his painting hat. It was covered with so much paint that you couldn't see the words anymore.

2 Dad looked grim. "No. We need a radio. I can't paint without some good painting music."

3 "I'll get the old one from the basement," Michelle called out as she ran into the house. When she got back, Dad stirred the paint. Then, he stared at the fence. It went all the way around the yard.

4 "On each post," Dad explained, "you have to do the front, then both side edges."

5 "The front, the edge, and the other edge," repeated Michelle. She made a little song out of it. Then, she sang it so many times she thought she would blow up. And there were still 472 posts to go!

1. Write **1**, **2**, and **3** by these sentences to show what happened first, next, and last.

_____ Dad stirred the paint.

_____ Michelle got the radio.

_____ Dad and Michelle painted.

2. What does Michelle have to do on each post?

_____

3. Why does Michelle think she will blow up?

_____

4. Have you ever done a task that went on and on and on? Write about it.

_____

5. In the second paragraph, why does Dad look grim?

_____

6. What does Dad's painting hat tell you about him?

_____

7. What can you learn about the story from the picture? Choose something that you didn't learn from the text.

_____

8. What does Dad send Michelle inside to do?

_____

Mixed Up Day

What goes wrong for Danny?

1 It all started at breakfast. The milk jumped out of the jug and flowed all over the table and all over me. I barely had time to clean up the table and put on a clean shirt.

2 On the way to school, I saw myself in a store window. Bed head! My hair was sticking up to the sky on one side, and the shirt I had on did not match my pants.

3 At school, I headed right to the water fountain so I could wet down my hair. I pushed the button. Nothing happened. I pushed again and looked closely to see what was wrong. All of a sudden, the water spurted up into my face. My hair was fixed, sort of, but now my shirt was soaked.

4 I slid into my desk, hoping no one would notice. Mr. Torres looked right at me. "Oh, Danny. Tomorrow is Mixed Up Day, not today."

Put each word in the right blank.

water	hair	milk

1. First, Danny spilled the _____.

2. Then, he had a problem with his _____.

3. Next, he got sprayed with _____.

4. What did Danny look like when he sat down in his desk?

_____

5. Have you ever had a mixed up day? Write about it.

_____

6. In the first paragraph, it says "the milk jumped out of the jug." What does this mean?

_____

7. How does Danny notice the problem with his hair and shirt?

_____

8. Write **T** for *true* or **F** for *false* next to each sentence below.

_____ Mr. Torres is Danny's teacher.

_____ Danny spilled orange juice on the table.

_____ Danny's dad drove him to school.

_____ The water fountain sprays Danny's shirt.

Mountain Magic

How does the girls' project turn out?

1 "Oh, we missed a spot," said Hailey, pointing.

2 "Okay," said Megan, dabbing at the spot. "Are we done now?" She and her best friend, Hailey, had made a volcano out of wet, sticky goop. They were painting it to look like a mountain.

3 The next day, they were ready for fun. Megan thought out loud, "Mrs. Metzer said the baking soda goes first, then the vinegar. Right?"

4 "That's right," said Megan's mom. "Are you ready for the lava?"

5 "Ready!" they said together.

6 In went the baking soda. The girls held their breath. In went the vinegar. It hit the soda and bubbled up, up, up, and over the edge of the volcano.

7 Megan and Hailey clapped. "Yea, it worked! Let's do it again!"

1. Write **1**, **2**, **3**, and **4** by these sentences to show what happened first, second, third, and last.

_____ The girls painted the volcano.

_____ The friends made a volcano.

_____ Bubbles came up out of the volcano.

_____ Baking soda and vinegar went into the volcano.

Some of these sentences are about **real** things. Write **R** by them. The other sentences are about **make believe** things. Write **M** by them.

2. _____ The girls can build a real volcano.

3. _____ A real volcano can be on someone's back porch.

4. _____ The girls do projects together.

5. _____ Mothers help with projects.

6. A mixture of two things makes the volcano bubble up. What two things do the girls use?

_____   _____

7. Who is Mrs. Metzer?

_____

8. Look at the picture. Why are the girls wearing goggles?

_____

9. Was the project a success? How do you know?

_____

Making Plans

Read to see what the Shaws are planning.

1 "Where will they sleep?" Lisa asked her mom. Lisa was wondering if she could fit two cousins in her bed without hurting any stuffed animals.

2 "They'll sleep in the green bedroom, just like last time," answered Mrs. Shaw.

3 Lisa was a little bit glad. "Oh, that's good," she said. Now, she had another question. "What will they do?" Lisa was wondering if she had enough dress-up clothes to go around.

4 "I'm not sure yet. They'll be here for a week. We'll have to plan some things," said Mrs. Shaw. "I thought we might spend one day at the zoo."

5 "I vote for the zoo, too," Lisa replied.

1. Who is coming to visit Lisa's family?

_____

2. Lisa's cousins won't be sleeping in her room. How does she feel about this? Why?

_____

3. What do you think will happen next in the story? Circle the correct answer.

Lisa and her brother will go to bed.

Lisa will hide her dress-up clothes.

The cousins will arrive.

4. Look at the picture. What is happening in the thought bubble over Lisa's head?

_____

5. How does the picture help you to understand the story better?

_____

Fill in the blank to complete each sentence below.

6. Lisa's cousins will be staying for _____.

7. Lisa doesn't want her stuffed animals to get _____.

8. Mrs. Shaw says that the family will visit the _____ one day.

9. The Shaws' extra bedroom is painted _____.

10. Lisa's _____ have visited before.

To the Zoo

What would you want to see at the zoo?

1 "Is everyone buckled in?" called Mrs. Shaw.

2 "Yes, Mom. Hold on, tigers. Here I come!" sang Jake from the back seat.

3 "Ooh, tigers? You didn't tell me there were tigers there," said Charlie. "Here we come!"

4 Julia was very grown-up. "I would rather spend my time looking at animals that don't want to eat me. I like to watch the owls."

5 "An owl would eat you if you were a mouse!" called Charlie. Julia made a face.

6 "What about you, Lisa?" Mrs. Shaw asked. "What do you want to see?"

7 "Make mine zebras," she answered, after thinking for a moment.

8 Mrs. Shaw laughed. "Zebras, tigers, and owls—oh, my!"

1. How does everyone feel about going to the zoo?

_____ They are tired.   _____ They are eager.

2. Why isn't Julia very interested in seeing the tigers?

_____

3. Write **first**, **next**, and **last** on the lines to show the order in which events happened.

_____ Lisa wants to see the zebras.

_____ Mrs. Shaw asks if everyone is buckled in.

_____ Julia makes a face.

4. What does Charlie say would happen if Julia were a mouse?

_____

5. How are Charlie and Julia related to each other?

_____

6. Is this story realistic, or is it a fantasy? Explain.

_____

7. What animals would you like to see if you went to the zoo?

_____

8. What was the author's purpose in writing this story?

_____ to entertain   _____ to make you want to visit the zoo

_____ to teach you about zoo animals

Zebra News

Read to learn about zebras.

Where Zebras Live

[1] Wild zebras live only in Africa. They choose open country that has some areas of trees and grass.

How Zebras Live

[2] Zebras move together in large groups called herds. They often travel with herds of other animals, such as antelopes, wildebeest, and gnus. Zebras graze, or eat grass. When the grass is gone in one area, the herd moves to another area.

Other Zebra News

[3] How can you tell one zebra from another? By their stripes, of course. Each zebra's stripes are different from every other zebra's stripes. The animals' stripes help them blend together when they are in a herd. That makes it harder for lions to single out and catch one zebra.

1. What is a large group of zebras called?

_____

2. Why does a herd move from place to place?

_____

_____

3. What are some other animals that move in groups?

_____

4. Why do zebras' stripes make it hard for lions to catch a zebra?

_____

_____

5. How are a zebra's stripes similar to a human's fingerprints?

_____

6. What animals are a threat to zebras?

_____

7. In what part of the world are zebras found?

_____

8. A zebra's stripes are a form of camouflage. What is another animal that uses camouflage? Explain.

_____

_____

Tiger Tips

Read to learn something new about tigers.

Where Tigers Live

1 You might find a tiger on a mountain, in a deep forest, or in a wet, grassy area. You will have to go to Asia, however, to find one in the wild.

How Tigers Live

2 If you're looking for a tiger in the middle of the day, look in cool places. Tigers stay out of the heat by sleeping in caves or by lying in thick grass or in shallow water. After a day of rest, the tiger is ready to hunt all night. Once a tiger catches its meal, it drags it to a quiet place to eat in peace.

Other Tiger Tips

3 If you're looking for a tiger cub, look for its mother. A mother tiger, or *tigress*, takes care of her cubs for more than two years. She protects them, brings them food, and teaches them how to hunt.

1. In what three kinds of places do tigers live?

_____

2. How are these places different?

_____

3. How does the author help you with the word tigress?

_____

_____

4. Under what heading can you find information about when a tiger hunts?

_____

5. What is similar about the way the articles on pages 246 and 248 are organized?

_____

6. In what kinds of places do tigers like to sleep?

_____

7. Tigers hunt at night. What other kinds of animals hunt at night? Think of at least two examples.

_____   _____

8. Is this article fiction or nonfiction? How do you know?

_____

_____

Only Owls

Read to find out about owls.

Feathers

1   Owls fly on silent wings. Their feathers are so soft that they make no noise during flight. How does that help an owl? It allows the owl to sneak up on its prey, or the animals it hunts and eats, such as mice, rats, rabbits, small birds, and insects.

Eyes and Ears

2   Does an owl see well with its large round eyes? Yes, especially at night. Owls also have excellent hearing. In fact, they use their hearing, rather than sight, to find their prey.

Feet

3   Why might a bird's feet be important? Owls have strong three-toed feet with sharp claws. To hunt, owls swoop down and catch their prey with their feet. Most owls then swallow their prey whole.

1. Do you think owls would be able to live in a city? Explain.

_____

_____

2. What would happen if an owl made noise as it flew?

_____

_____

3. What do the three headings have in common?

_____

_____

4. Why are an owl's feet important for hunting?

_____

_____

5. Why does the author say, "An owl flies on silent wings"?

_____

6. Based on the text, what is prey?

_____

7. Which two senses are most important to an owl for hunting?

_____   _____

8. Name three animals that owls eat.

_____   _____   _____

Remembering the Zoo

What did the children like about the zoo?

1 "I wish I could sleep just like that big, old tiger," said Charlie. They had had a great day at the zoo, but he sure was tired. He remembered the tigers and smiled though.

2 "He was lying in the dirt," said Julia, making a face. "I would like to be up on a high branch. That's where wise animals sleep." She thought of the owls and smiled.

3 Jake was still ready for action. "Not me," he spoke up. "I'm glad one of the tigers was awake. I wish I could climb rocks like he did." Everyone nodded, thinking about the strong animal and how easily he had moved.

4 After a long time, Lisa had a question. "Mom?" she asked in a small voice. "Do you think I would look good in stripes?"

1. Why didn't Julia care for the sleeping tiger?

_____

2. Why does Lisa want stripes?

_____

_____

Some of these sentences are about **real** things. Write **R** by them. The other sentences are about **make believe** things. Write **M** by them.

3. _____ Animals ride in car seats.

4. _____ Children sleep in beds.

5. _____ People climb rocks.

6. _____ Girls perch in trees.

7. Why does Julia think that owls are wise?

_____

8. What do you think Charlie's favorite part of the zoo visit was?

_____

9. What did the tiger do that the kids admired?

_____ roared   _____ climbed rocks   _____ slept

10. Do you think the kids will want to visit the zoo again? Why or why not?

_____

_____

Waving Good Bye

What does the boy remember about his grandparents' visit?

1   I stood on the porch for a long time and waved. Gram and Gramps had such a long drive. They wouldn't get home until tomorrow.

2   Everything seemed quiet now that they were gone. Gramps wasn't telling one of his stories. The best one was about the fort he and his brothers had built in the hay barn. It seemed as if the fort got bigger every time I heard the story.

3   And Gram wasn't in the kitchen humming like she always did. Every now and then, she would even dance a little. Then, she'd look up and laugh. If anyone was watching, her face would turn red.

4   I watched until their car was just a dot. Then, I hummed a little song and went to ask my dad about the hay in the barn.

1. Which word best describes the boy's feelings about his grandparents?

fond   excited   hopeless

2. Why do you think the fort "got bigger" every time Gramps told the story?

_____

3. What do you think the boy might do next?

_____

4. Mark the sentence that is true.

_____ Gramps grew up on a farm.

_____ Gramps grew up in the city.

5. What information in the story helped you answer question **4**?

_____

6. Who is telling the story?

_____ Gramps   _____ the boy   _____ the boy's dad

7. Read the two sentences below. Write **C** for *cause* next to one and **E** for *effect* next to the other.

_____ Gram and Gramps have headed home.

_____ Everything seems quiet now.

8. Why do you think Gram's face sometimes turns red?

_____

Games for a Rainy Day

What do Gina and her mom do on a rainy day?

1   *Rumble, rumble, rumble.* The afternoon thunder told me that we would not get to go swimming this afternoon. I went looking for my mom just as the first raindrops fell.

2   "What can I do, Mom?"

3   Mom looked up from her book. I saw her eyes move to the window, and then she frowned. "Hmm," she said, "this looks like a day for the game closet, Gina. How about pick-up sticks? Or hopscotch?"

4   I groaned. Those were little kid games. "Uh, anything else?" I asked hopefully.

5   Mom shook her head. "Those are good games. Let's try them." We headed for the closet.

6   Mom and I played all afternoon. Once we laughed until we fell over. It was pretty fun, even if they were little kid games.

1. Gina knows she will not be able to swim this afternoon because

_____ .

2. Mom frowned because _____ .

3. This story is mostly about

_____ the rules for playing hopscotch.

_____ cleaning out a closet full of games.

_____ how a girl and her mom spend an afternoon.

4. Why didn't Gina like her mom's ideas at first?

_____

5. How did the afternoon turn out for Gina?

_____

_____

6. If the next day is sunny, what do you think Gina and her mom will do?

_____

7. What is the setting for this story?

_____

8. What games do you like to play on rainy afternoons?

_____

_____

Clouds and Rain Today

Read to find out why it rains.

1 Water is all around us—in lakes, rivers, streams, oceans, and even puddles. Heat from the sun causes tiny parts of that water to rise into the air. Those tiny parts are called *water vapor*.

2 Up in the air, the water vapor forms clouds. The tiny parts of water in the vapor join to form small drops of water in the clouds. These drops may freeze as the clouds rise. The higher they go, the colder the air becomes.

3 When the water drops in the cloud get too heavy, they fall back to the ground. The water falls as rain, snow, hail, or sleet. Some of the water flows back into rivers, streams, and the ocean. The next time the sun shines, the cycle starts all over again.

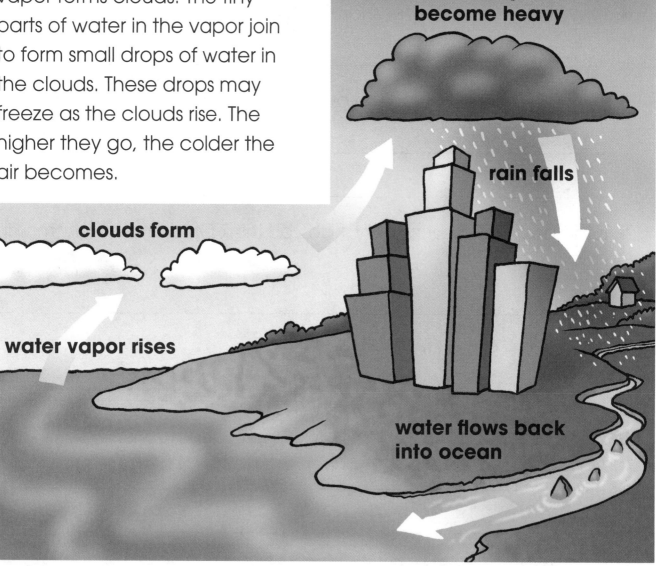

water drops become heavy

rain falls

clouds form

water vapor rises

water flows back into ocean

1. Write **1**, **2**, **3**, and **4** by these sentences to show the correct order of the steps in the water cycle.

_____ Rain, snow, hail, or sleet falls to the ground.

_____ Water vapor rises and forms clouds.

_____ The sun's heat causes water to form water vapor.

_____ Water drops form and become heavy.

2. Look at the picture of the water cycle. What do the arrows above the ocean tell you?

_____

3. Explain the water cycle in your own words.

_____

_____

4. What happens when the water drops in a cloud get too heavy?

_____

5. What rises up into the air to form clouds?

_____ water vapor   _____ hail   _____ snow

6. Name three places you can find water in nature.

_____   _____   _____

7. Here is an effect: **Water vapor rises into the air.** What is the cause?

_____

Shopping with Dad

What does Gina learn at the store?

1 I like shopping with my dad. The other day, we went to the grocery store. I laughed so hard I almost fell over. I learned omething, too. It all started when Dad got excited about the corn on the cob.

2 "What's the big deal? There is fresh food here all the time," I said.

3 "Yes, that's true, Gina," agreed Dad, "but it's nice to see fresh food that was grown nearby. Then, we know it's really fresh."

4 "Oh," I said. I guess Dad could tell I didn't get it. He explained.

5 "Some of the fresh food was picked many days ago, maybe even weeks ago. Then, it probably got washed, put into packages, loaded onto a truck, and unloaded here."

6 "Oh," I said. We chose six ears. It was the best corn I ever ate. Now I get it.

1. Why does Gina's dad get excited about the corn?

_____

2. Why isn't some of the fresh food really fresh?

_____

_____

3. What does Gina's dad do that makes her laugh?

_____

4. Where did you find the answer to question 3?

_____

5. Tell two things you know about Dad from reading the story.

_____

_____

6. What does Gina think about the corn after she eats it?

_____

7. Read each sentence. If it is a fact, write **F** on the line. If it is an opinion, write **O**.

_____ It was the best corn I ever ate.

_____ It's nice to see fresh food that was grown nearby.

_____ We chose six ears.

Backyard Corn

Learn how to grow corn by reading the passage below.

1   Corn is fairly easy to grow. Even in a small backyard garden, a family can grow enough corn for quite a number of yummy meals.

2   First, take care of the soil, just like for any garden. Work it up as deeply as you can. Chop up clumps of dirt, and rake the surface smooth.

3   Next comes the planting. Place seeds 2 inches deep and about 12 inches apart.

Your rows should be about 2 feet apart. Keep the soil moist. You'll have to wait for 10 to 15 days for the seeds to sprout. Once they do sprout, water them (if it doesn't rain), and keep the rows clear of weeds.

4   About 70 to 90 days after you plant your corn seeds, you will be able to enjoy your first harvest. Pass the butter and the salt, please!

Write these steps in the correct order.

- watch plants grow
- plant seeds
- water soil
- harvest corn
- prepare soil

1. _____

2. _____

3. _____

4. _____

5. _____

6. At the end of the article, why does the author say, "Pass the butter and the salt, please"?

_____

7. What is the main idea of paragraph 2?

_____

8. It takes the seeds _____ to _____ days to sprout.

9. Based on the text, how do you think the author feels about growing corn?

_____

10. If you could choose to grow something in a garden, what would it be? Why?

_____

_____

Corn: How We Use It

What are some different uses of corn?

1 There was a time when the only use for corn was to eat it or to feed it to the cattle or hogs. Those days are long gone.

2 There may be as many as four thousand products at your grocery store that contain corn. No, they're not putting corn kernels in your peanut butter. But they might be sweetening the peanut butter with corn syrup. And there may be another corn product—corn starch—in items such as baked goods and laundry soaps. If you drive home from the store, you could use a fuel made from corn called *ethanol*.

3 About half of the corn that American farmers grow is still fed to cattle and hogs. The other half, though, shows up in everything from paper to shampoo, from medicine to the glue on a postage stamp.

1. Today, corn is used in thousands of products. How is that different from many years ago?

_____

2. The article mentions two food products that come from corn. What are they?

_____   _____

3. Half of the corn grown in America is fed to cattle and hogs. Why is that important?

_____

4. What are two ways to use corn, aside from eating it?

_____

5. What is the author's purpose for writing this article?

_____ to get people to buy more corn

_____ to teach about the uses of corn

_____ to make you laugh

6. Corn is no longer fed to farm animals. Is this true or false?

_____

7. Do you think ethanol is a good way to power cars? Why or why not?

_____

_____

Something New for Gina

Read to see what Gina learns at the picnic.

1 Tonight was the Nolan Street picnic. We have one every year. Everyone brings one dish of food. Then, you go along the table and you wonder what to try because some of it looks sort of unusual.

2 "Gina, don't you want some of this salad? It has raisins in it." Mom never gives up.

3 "Um, no, thanks, Mom. I took some apple slices for my salad." I took other safe things, such as potato salad and baked beans. Then, my dad came up all of a sudden.

4 "Gina, try this pizza. It is great!" he said. Before I could say anything, he popped a piece into my mouth.

5 "Hey, Dad! This isn't pizza."

6 "Ah, but it is. It's fruit pizza," he said, grinning.

7 I asked for another piece. Then, I asked Mrs. Taylor for the recipe.

1. Explain how the Nolan Street picnic works.

_____

_____

2. Who do you think made the fruit pizza?

_____

3. Which of these sentences best tells how Gina feels about food?

_____ If it's food, I'll try it.

_____ I like to try new foods.

_____ I'll try something only if I know what it is.

_____ I like trying foods that have fruit in them.

4. Did Gina like the fruit pizza? How could you tell?

_____

5. In paragraph 3, Gina says she took "safe things." What do you think she means by "safe"?

_____

6. Who does Gina go to the picnic with?

_____

7. Do you enjoy trying new foods? Explain.

_____

_____

Fruit Pizza

Does this sound like something you would like to try?

Ingredients

- 1 package (20 ounces) sugar cookie dough

- 8 ounces cream cheese, softened

- $\frac{1}{3}$ cup sugar

- $\frac{1}{2}$ teaspoon vanilla extract

- $\frac{1}{2}$ cup orange marmalade

- 2 tablespoons water

- 4–6 types of fruit (bananas, oranges, blueberries, seedless grapes, strawberries, and so on)

Directions

1 On a cookie sheet or pizza pan, press cookie dough into a thin circle about 12 inches wide. Bake at 375° F for 12 minutes or until golden brown. Cool. Place on serving tray.

2 Combine cream cheese, sugar, and vanilla. Mix until well blended. Spread over crust. Slice and arrange fruit over cream cheese mixture. Mix marmalade and water. Pour over fruit. Chill. Cut into wedges to serve.

Write these steps in the correct order. (Not all of the recipe's steps are here.)

- chill
- bake dough
- press dough into circle
- slice and arrange fruit
- make cream cheese mixture

1. _____

2. _____

3. _____

4. _____

5. _____

Recipes often use short forms of words called **abbreviations**. Match the abbreviations in the box with their common recipe words.

c.	oz.	tsp.	pkg.

6. teaspoon _____

7. cup _____

8. ounce _____

9. package _____

10. What step do you have to do after you bake the pizza dough, before you add the spread?

_____ arrange the fruit   _____ cool it

_____ cut it into wedges

New Neighbors

Read to see what Yuki discovers.

1   The grass looked shiny. It had rained last night, but now the sun was shining brightly. If Yuki looked just right, she could even see little sparkles. She waded out into the grass to see if she could catch one.

2   Just as she bent down near a sparkle, she saw a girl looking at her over the fence. Yuki stopped. The girl waved her fingers a little bit. Yuki waved back a little bit and stood up.

3   Just then, Yuki's mom stepped out the back door. "Oh, hello. Yuki, this must be Roxie. I was just talking to her mom in the front yard." The girl nodded.

4   "Do you want to see my sunflowers?" asked Roxie. Yuki looked at her mom, and then nodded. She went to the fence. In the corner of Roxie's yard, she saw the tallest flowers she had ever seen in her whole life.

1. This story is mostly about

_____ a girl playing in the wet grass.

_____ how a rain storm hurt some plants.

_____ two neighbor girls and how they meet.

2. What do you think will happen next in the story?

_____

_____

Use the story to fill in the blanks and complete each sentence.

3. Roxie likes to grow _____.

4. Yuki is looking at raindrops on the _____.

5. Roxie and Yuki are on opposite sides of the _____.

6. Yuki's mom has already met Roxie's _____.

7. In what season do you think this story takes place? Explain your answer.

_____

_____

_____

8. What are two adjectives you could use to describe the grass in the yard?

_____   _____

The Sunflower House

Can you imagine a sunflower house?

Follow these directions to make your own sunflower house.

1. Choose a sunny space for a garden. Get permission from a grown-up to use the space.

2. Lay down a string to outline your garden. You may make a round or square space.

3. Dig a small ditch around the inside of your string. You may need a grown-up to help. Chop or rake the soil so it is fine and smooth.

4. In your ditch, place one sunflower seed about every nine inches. Go all the way around the circle. Then, remove one seed. That spot will be your doorway.

5. Brush soil over the seeds with your fingers. Press gently all around the ditch. Then, water and wait for your house to grow.

6 inches

5 feet

1. What did you think of when you read the title, "The Sunflower House"?

_____

2. Was your idea anything like the sunflower house described in the directions? Explain.

_____

3. What information is given only in the diagram?

_____

4. Would you have been able to follow the directions without the diagram? Explain.

_____

5. Do sunflowers need a sunny or shady place to grow?

_____

6. For which part will you probably need a grown-up's help?

_____

7. How far apart should you plant the seeds?

_____

8. Why do you remove one seed before you cover the rest with dirt?

_____

Math Grade 2 Answers

Chapter 1

Lesson 1.1, page 6
3 + 3 = 6; 5 + 5 + 5 + 5 = 20
4 + 4 + 4 = 12; 1 + 1 + 1 + 1 + 1 = 5
3 + 3 + 3 = 9; 4 + 4 = 8

Lesson 1.1, page 7
2 + 2 = 4; 4 + 4 + 4 + 4 = 16
1 + 1 = 2; 5 + 5 + 5 = 15
5 + 5 + 5 + 5 + 5 = 25; 5 + 5 = 10

Lesson 1.2, page 8
8, 14
15, 20, 30, 35
40, 50, 60
14, 16, 22
20, 30, 35, 55, 65, 75, 80
80, 60, 40, 30

Lesson 1.3, page 9
8, 10, 12
84, 88, 90
10, 20, 30

Lesson 1.3, page 10
55, 65, 75
20, 40, 50, 80, 90
80, 60, 40, 30, 20

Lesson 1.4, page 11
8, even, 4 + 4 = 8; 5, odd

Lesson 1.4, page 12

8, 4 + 4 = 8, even; 3, odd
7, odd; 6, 3 + 3 = 6, even

Chapter 2

Lesson 2.1, page 13
5, 4, 5, 4, 1, 3
2, 2, 5, 3, 4, 3
4, 0, 5, 4, 4, 2
1, 5, 3, 4, 5, 2
0, 2, 5, 3, 4, 5

Lesson 2.2, page 14
3, 0, 0, 1, 3, 3
0, 1, 0, 1, 2, 4
4, 2, 2, 0, 2, 3
1, 5, 0, 3, 0, 0
1, 3, 1, 2, 3, 4

Lesson 2.3, page 15
6, 8, 7, 7, 8, 8
6, 6, 7, 6, 8, 8
7, 7, 8, 7, 6, 6
8, 8, 7, 8, 6, 7
8, 8, 7, 6, 6, 7

Lesson 2.4, page 16
4, 6, 3, 4, 3, 4
7, 1, 2, 0, 5, 0
5, 6, 3, 1, 2, 2
0, 6, 5, 7, 8, 1
4, 5, 4, 4, 0, 3

Lesson 2.5, page 17
9, 10, 10, 9, 10, 9
9, 9, 10, 10, 10, 9
9, 9, 9, 9, 9, 10
9, 10, 10, 10, 9, 9
9, 10, 10, 10, 10, 9

Lesson 2.6, page 18
3, 5, 6, 6, 1, 2
9, 1, 4, 2, 8, 4
9, 5, 3, 7, 7, 10
0, 8, 6, 1, 9, 4
1, 5, 8, 2, 2, 7

Lesson 2.7, page 19
12, 11, 13, 11, 12, 11
12, 13, 12, 12, 11, 13
11, 12, 11, 13, 11, 13
13, 11, 12, 12, 13, 11
11, 12, 12, 13, 13, 11

Lesson 2.8, page 20
8, 2, 4, 7, 9, 5
3, 7, 5, 9, 6, 6
9, 4, 3, 8, 6, 8
7, 8, 4, 6, 7, 4
9, 7, 3, 9, 5, 5

Math Grade 2 Answers

Lesson 2.9, page 21
14, 12, 16, 13, 14, 11
11, 14, 13, 16, 12, 16
14, 15, 12, 11, 14, 13
15, 12, 12, 11, 15, 15
13, 14, 11, 16, 11 ,14

Lesson 2.10, page 22
5, 7, 5, 8, 7, 4
5, 9, 6, 7, 9, 6
9, 7, 8, 2, 6, 8
4, 3, 6, 8, 9, 9
7, 7, 5, 8, 5, 7

Lesson 2.11, page 23
18, 17, 16, 13, 19, 12
14, 20, 15, 12, 15, 17
17, 14, 12, 13, 12, 14
19, 13, 18, 15 ,12 ,20
20, 14, 13, 17, 16, 19

Lesson 2.12, page 24
9, 8, 6, 8, 6, 11
3, 9, 8, 5, 7, 6
8, 6, 8, 12, 5, 9
8, 9, 5, 4, 16, 7
15, 9, 9, 4, 7, 10

Lesson 2.13, page 25

$$\begin{array}{r} 13 \\ -\ 7 \\ \hline 6 \end{array}$$

$$\begin{array}{r} 8 \\ +\ 6 \\ \hline 14 \end{array}$$

$$\begin{array}{r} 15 \\ -\ 7 \\ \hline 8 \end{array}$$

$$\begin{array}{r} 6 \\ +\ 3 \\ \hline 9 \end{array}$$

$$\begin{array}{r} 18 \\ -\ 9 \\ \hline 9 \end{array}$$

Chapter 3

Lesson 3.1, page 26
64, 79, 79, 87, 74
76, 48, 87, 94, 88
91, 89, 98, 69, 89
87, 69, 85, 79, 59
95, 77, 98, 59, 53

Lesson 3.2, page 27
10, 81, 12, 14, 52
16, 53, 30, 12, 15
21, 14, 33, 24, 26
11, 30, 60, 31, 22
5, 14, 10, 62, 5

Lesson 3.3, page 28

$$\begin{array}{r} 28 \\ -10 \\ \hline 18 \end{array}$$

$$\begin{array}{r} 32 \\ -30 \\ \hline 2 \end{array}$$

$$\begin{array}{r} 65 \\ -22 \\ \hline 43 \end{array}$$

$$\begin{array}{r} 59 \\ -44 \\ \hline 15 \end{array}$$

$$\begin{array}{r} 37 \\ -12 \\ \hline 25 \end{array}$$

Lesson 3.4, page 29
69, 88, 87, 68, 96
87, 49, 87, 65, 59
69, 56, 58, 47, 66
79, 39, 77, 68, 88

Lesson 3.5, page 30

$$\begin{array}{r} 10 \\ 12 \\ +25 \\ \hline 47 \end{array}$$

$$\begin{array}{r} 14 \\ 15 \\ +20 \\ \hline 49 \end{array}$$

Math Grade 2 Answers

```
    6
   22
  +30
  ‾‾‾‾
   58

   32
   26
  +10
  ‾‾‾‾
   68

   14
   23
  +30
  ‾‾‾‾
   67
```

```
   25        52
  +27       -19
  ‾‾‾‾      ‾‾‾‾
   52       (33)

   31
  - 8
  ‾‾‾‾
   23

   26
  -(8)
  ‾‾‾‾
   18

   42
  -27
  ‾‾‾‾
   15
```

Chapter 4

Lesson 4.1, page 31

81, 92, 64, 37, 82
92, 96, 84, 81, 36
72, 62, 51, 92, 85
70, 73, 70, 30, 91

Lesson 4.2, page 32

```
   35
  +39
  ‾‾‾‾
   74

   48        84
  +36       -30
  ‾‾‾‾      ‾‾‾‾
   84       (54)

   33
  +28
  ‾‾‾‾
   61

    9
  +(15)
  ‾‾‾‾
   24

   15
  +16
  ‾‾‾‾
   31
```

Lesson 4.3, page 33

29, 12, 29, 37, 7
57, 12, 27, 9, 57
15, 37, 5, 21, 19
38, 15, 15, 28, 56

Lesson 4.4, page 34

```
   33
  -28
  ‾‾‾‾
    5
```

Chapter 5

Lesson 5.1, page 35

165, 100 + 60 + 5; 178, 100 + 70 +8
184, 100 + 80 + 4; 158, 100 + 50 + 8
170, 100 + 70; 152, 100 + 50 + 2
180, 100 + 80; 161, 100 + 60 + 1

Lesson 5.2, page 36

235, two hundred thirty five; 309, three hundred nine
324, three hundred twenty four; 217,
   two hundred seventeen
390, three hundred ninety; 289, two hundred eighty nine
241, two hundred forty one; 307, three hundred seven

Lesson 5.3, page 37

542, five hundred forty two; 435, four hundred thirty five
640, six hundred forty; 514, five hundred fourteen
494, four hundred ninety four; 671,
   six hundred seventy one
433, four hundred thirty three; 508, five hundred eight

Lesson 5.4, page 38

722, 700 + 20 + 2
956, 900 + 50 + 6; 809, 800 + 9
840, 800 + 40
774, 700 + 70 + 4; 963, 900 + 60 + 3
917, 900 + 10 + 7

Lesson 5.5, page 39

313, 315, 316
417, 419, 421
610, 615, 620, 635
785, 795, 810 ,815
210, 220, 240, 260
360, 380, 390, 410, 420
200, 400, 500, 700
700, 600, 400, 300

Math Grade 2 Answers

Lesson 5.5, page 40
410, 415, 420, 435, 440
320, 330, 340, 370
660, 650, 640, 610
502, 492, 472, 462
440, 540, 740, 840
210, 310, 510, 610, 710
850, 750, 650, 550, 350
726, 626, 426, 326

Lesson 5.6, page 41
831 < 843; 436 > 379; 902 < 911
567 > 564; 306 < 401; 535 = 535
219 > 198; 739 > 730; 630 < 820
127 > 119; 407 < 610; 923 < 925
354 < 453; 802 > 792; 236 < 401
504 = 504; 402 < 408; 123 > 118
367 < 562; 760 > 740; 654 < 736
981 > 901; 391 < 491; 835 > 830

Lesson 5.7, page 42
140; 61; 151; 111; 94
81; 110; 104; 111; 121
141; 44; 120; 93; 91
81; 134; 121; 94; 62
43; 101; 80; 141; 127
114; 122; 120; 94; 88

Lesson 5.8, page 43
685; 1,153; 933; 1,123; 444
1,175; 1,030; 1,570; 1,042; 1,280
1,282; 1,001; 681; 973; 1,356
982; 944; 367; 404; 414
1,424; 850; 1,378; 1,350; 446
1,334; 1,070; 880; 1,251; 1,125

Lesson 5.9, page 44
212; 593; 489; 120; 480
408; 206; 279; 106; 377
331; 399; 519; 189; 577
114; 208; 529; 171; 448
86; 627; 25; 350; 86
281; 349; 225; 336; 129

Lesson 5.10, page 45
369; 901; 417; 732; 521
1,108; 606; 1,075; 1,005; 397
847; 711; 931; 550; 531
1,055; 589; 812; 902; 382

Lesson 5.11, page 46
570; 238; 33; 326; 165;
121; 15; 226; 112; 129;
399; 220; 106; 263; 264
187; 462; 437; 303; 215

Chapter 6

Lesson 6.1, page 47
7, 7:00; 12, 12:00; 11, 11:00
10, 10:00; 6, 6:00; 5, 5:00
9, 9:00; 8, 8:00; 2, 2:00

Lesson 6.2, page 48
4, 4:30; 10, 10:30; 11, 11:30
2, 2:30; 1, 1:30; 6, 6:30
5, 5:30; 9, 9:30; 3, 3:30

Lesson 6.3, page 49
6:45; 5:15; 10:15
3:45; 11:15; 7:45

Lesson 6.3, page 50
3, 4; 6; 3:30
5, 6; 9; 5:45
8; 12; 8:00
10, 11; 3; 10:15
4; 12; 4:00

Lesson 6.4, page 51
Check student's estimates against actual lengths: 5 in., 4 in., 2 in., 7 in., 3 in.

Lesson 6.5, page 52
Check student's estimates against actual lengths: 6 cm, 5 cm, 9 cm, 12 cm, 9 cm

Lesson 6.6, page 53
3 in.
5 in.
3 in.; 2 in.
6 in.
1 in.; 3 in.

Lesson 6.7, page 54
1; 1; 2; 0; 1; 1

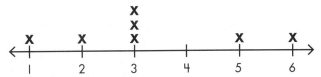

Lesson 6.8, page 55
1 in.; 5 in.
2 in.; 4 in.
3, 1, 3, 1, 8 in.; 2, 2, 2, 6 in.
1, 1, 1, 1, 4 in.; 2, 1, 2, 1, 6 in.

Lesson 6.9, page 56

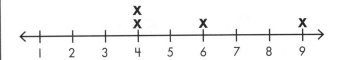

Math Grade 2 Answers

Lesson 6.10, page 57

8 cm; 4 cm
6 cm
7 cm; 9 cm
17 cm

Lesson 6.11, page 58

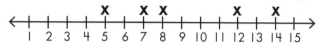

Lesson 6.12, page 59

6 cm; 5 cm
2 cm; 9 cm
6, 2, 6, 2, 16 cm; 6, 1, 6, 1, 14 cm
4, 4, 4, 4, 16 cm; 3, 3, 3, 3, 3, 15 cm

Lesson 6.13, page 60

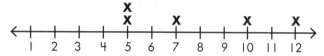

Lesson 6.14, page 61

3 in., 2 in., 1 in. longer
5 in., 3 in., 2 in. longer
1 in., 2 in., 1 in. longer
3 in., 5 in., 2 in. longer

Lesson 6.14, page 62

6 cm, 4 cm, 2 cm longer
8 cm, 4 cm, 4 cm longer
4 cm, 5 cm, 1 cm longer
7 cm, 6 cm, 1 cm longer

Lesson 6.15, page 63

11 centimeters, 22 squares
14 centimeters, 28 squares
7 centimeters, 14 squares
15 centimeters, 30 squares
Answers may vary, but students should understand that the measurements in centimeters have lower numbers than those in squares.
Answers may vary, but students should understand that the squares are smaller units than centimeters.

Lesson 6.15, page 64

2 centimeters, about 1 inch
5 centimeters, about 2 inches
10 centimeters, about 4 inches
8 centimeters, about 3 inches
16 centimeters, about 6 inches
13 centimeters, about 5 inches

Answers may vary, but students should understand that the measurements in centimeters have higher numbers than those in inches.
Answers may vary, but students should understand that centimeters are smaller units than inches.

Lesson 6.16, page 65

$$\begin{array}{r} 48 \text{ ft.} \\ +21 \text{ ft.} \\ \hline 69 \text{ ft.} \end{array}$$

$$\begin{array}{r} 27 \text{ in.} \\ -11 \text{ in.} \\ \hline 16 \text{ in.} \end{array}$$

$$\begin{array}{r} 20 \text{ ft.} \\ -13 \text{ ft.} \\ \hline 7 \text{ ft.} \end{array}$$

$$\begin{array}{r} 25 \text{ in.} \\ -17 \text{ in.} \\ \hline 8 \text{ in.} \end{array}$$

$$\begin{array}{r} 70 \text{ in.} \\ -55 \text{ in.} \\ \hline 15 \text{ in.} \end{array}$$

Lesson 6.17, page 66

14
4
cat
7
25

Lesson 6.17, page 67

10
7
oranges
15
1
21

Lesson 6.17, page 68

40
12
Trina
11
17
5

Math Grade 2 Answers

Lesson 6.18, page 69

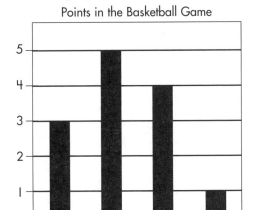
Points in the Basketball Game

Evan; Hugo; 13; 4

Lesson 6.19, page 70
Check student's picture graphs.

Shapes Around the Room	
Triangles	▲▲▲▲▲▲▲
Stars	☆☆☆☆☆☆☆☆☆☆
Squares	■■■■■■■■■
Circles	○○○○○○

star; circle; 3; 3

Lesson 6.20, page 71
30; 35; 65; 73

Chapter 7

Lesson 7.1, page 72
circle; rectangle; triangle; pentagon
hexagon; square; hexagon; square
square
hexagon
circle
triangle

Lesson 7.2, page 73

square pyramid
rectangular solid
sphere
cube

Lesson 7.3, page 74

Lesson 7.4, page 75
square and triangle
square
rectangle and square
circle

Chapter 8

Lesson 8.1, page 76
$\frac{3}{3}$, three-thirds; $\frac{2}{2}$, two-halves
$\frac{2}{2}$, two-halves; $\frac{3}{3}$, three-thirds
$\frac{4}{4}$, four-fourths; $\frac{4}{4}$, four-fourths

Math Grade 2 Answers

Lesson 8.2, page 77

2, 1, $\frac{1}{2}$; 2, 1, $\frac{1}{2}$

2, 1, $\frac{1}{2}$; 2, 1, $\frac{1}{2}$

One-half; One-half

Lesson 8.3, page 78

3, 1, $\frac{1}{3}$; 3, 1, $\frac{1}{3}$

3, 1, $\frac{1}{3}$; 3, 1, $\frac{1}{3}$

One-third; One-third

Lesson 8.4, page 79

4, 1, $\frac{1}{4}$; 4, 1, $\frac{1}{4}$

4, 1, $\frac{1}{4}$; 4, 1, $\frac{1}{4}$

One-fourth; One-fourth

Lesson 8.5, page 80

9; 12; 8

10; 12; 4

16; 12; 20

Language Arts Grade 2 Answers

Lesson 1.1   Common and Collective Nouns

A **noun** is a word that names a person, a place, or a thing.

    brother (person)   park (place)   bicycle (thing)

The nouns in the following sentences are in bold.

    The **teacher** gave us **work** to do.

    The **library** is next to the **pool**.

A **collective noun** is a word for a group of animals, things, or people.

    a **herd** of horses   a **deck** of cards   a **troupe** of actors

Identify It

Read the paragraph below. Circle each noun. There are 20 nouns.

I packed my (bag) for (camp.) I packed (shirts,) (shorts,) (socks,) and (shoes.) I added my (toothbrush) and a (comb.) My (mom) said to bring a (hat.) My (dad) said to bring a (game) and a (book.) I wanted to bring my (cat.) My (mom) and (dad) said (cats) do not go to (camp.) I brought a (photo) of my (cat) instead.

82

Lesson 1.1   Common and Collective Nouns

Complete It

A collective noun is missing from each sentence below. Fill in each blank with a noun from the box.

fleet	litter	school
flock	team	pod

1. A ___flock___ of birds landed in the apple tree.
2. Grace's cat gave birth to a ___litter___ of six kittens.
3. A ___fleet___ of ships left the harbor at noon.
4. The ___team___ of hockey players boarded the bus.
5. The shark spotted a ___school___ of fish.
6. A ___pod___ of dolphins leaped around the boat.

Try It

Write two sentences about what you would pack if you were going on a trip. Each sentence should have two nouns. Circle each noun.

1. ___Answers will vary.___
2. ___Answers will vary.___

83

Lesson 1.2   Proper Nouns

A **proper noun** is a noun that names a special person, place, or thing. Proper nouns begin with a capital letter to show that they are important. Here are some common and proper nouns.

Common Nouns	Proper Nouns
school	Thomas Jefferson Elementary School
sister	Emily
city	Capital City
dog	Bailey

Identify It

Read each sentence below. Underline the nouns. Write the letter **C** above each common noun. Write the letter **P** above each proper noun.

1. The <u>students</u>(C) in my <u>class</u>(C) are going on a <u>trip</u>(C).
2. We are going to the <u>New England Museum</u>(P).
3. I am going to sit near <u>Carson</u>(P), <u>Maddy</u>(P), and <u>Maria</u>(P) on the <u>bus</u>(C).
4. <u>Mr. Cohen</u>(P) said that we will have <u>lunch</u>(C) in the <u>cafeteria</u>(C).
5. My <u>family</u>(C) and I visited a <u>museum</u>(C) when we went to <u>Chicago</u>(P).

84

Lesson 1.2   Proper Nouns

Proof It

Read the paragraph below. Remember, proper nouns begin with a capital letter. If they do not, underline the first letter three times. Then, write the capital letter above it.

Example: Max and <u>e</u>(E)nrique went to <u>b</u>(B)uxton Public Library after school.

Chicago is the largest city in <u>i</u>(I)llinois. It is near the shores of <u>l</u>(L)ake <u>m</u>(M)ichigan. Aunt <u>s</u>(S)uzanne lives there. My sister, <u>e</u>(E)llie, loves to visit her in <u>c</u>(C)hicago. They like to go to the museums. Uncle <u>a</u>(A)lex said I can come visit next time.

Try It

1. Write a sentence that tells about a place you have visited. Your sentence should contain one proper noun. Circle the proper noun.

    ___Answers will vary.___

2. Now, write a sentence that tells about a place you would like to visit one day. It should also tell who you would like to bring along. Your sentence should contain two proper nouns. Circle the proper nouns.

    ___Answers will vary.___

85

Language Arts Grade 2 Answers

NAME_____

Lesson 1.3 Pronouns

A **pronoun** is a word that takes the place of a noun. Some pronouns are **I, me, you, he, she, him, her, it, we, us, they,** and **them.**

In the sentences below, pronouns take the place of the underlined nouns.

Drew and Lei play softball every Saturday.
They play softball every Saturday.

Dad parked the car in the garage.
Dad parked **it** in the garage.

Reflexive pronouns end in **self** or **selves.**
Myself, yourself, himself, herself, itself, ourselves, and **themselves** are reflexive pronouns.

Identify It

Circle the pronouns in the following paragraph. There are 12 pronouns.

(I) will never forget the first soccer game (I) ever saw. Mom, Dad, Laura, and (I) drove downtown to the stadium. (It) was lit up against the night sky. (We) were excited to see the Rangers play. The stadium was filled with hundreds of people. (They) cheered when the players ran onto the field. Laura and (I) screamed and clapped (ourselves) silly. (We) laughed when the Rangers' mascot did a funny dance. The best part of the game was when Matt Ramos scored the winning goal. (He) is the best player on the team. (It) was a night to remember for (myself) and my family!

86

NAME_____

Lesson 1.3 Pronouns

Complete It

Read each pair of sentences below. Choose the correct pronoun from the pair in parentheses ( ) to take the place of the underlined word or words. Write it in the space.

1. Mom drove Anna to soccer practice. Mom drove ___her___ (you, her) to soccer practice.

2. Dan and Marco are on Anna's team. ___They___ (Him, They) are on Anna's team.

3. Anna kicked the ball out of bounds. ___She___ (She, Her) kicked the ball out of bounds.

4. The coach talked to the players. The coach talked to ___them___ (she, them).

Rewrite It

Fill in each blank below with a reflexive pronoun.

1. The team served ___themselves___ a snack after the game.

2. Anna cut ___herself___ when she tripped over a rock.

3. Tim blamed ___himself___ for not checking the field better.

4. "You should be proud of ___yourselves___ for a great game!" said Coach.

87

NAME_____

Lesson 1.4 Verbs

Verbs are an important part of speech. They are often action words. They tell what happens in a sentence. The verbs in the sentences below are in bold.

Sadie **raced** down the stairs. She **barked** at the cat on the windowsill. Then, she **wagged** her tail at Mrs. Callahan. Sadie **ate** the treat from Mrs. Callahan's hand.

Solve It

Find the verb in each sentence. Write it in the spaces under the sentence.

1. Akiko placed her new puppy on the rug in the living room.
   p l (a) c e d

2. The puppy sniffed the rug and the couch.
   s (n) i f f e d

3. The puppy ran in circles around the room.
   r a (n)

4. Akiko and her dad giggled at the excited little dog.
   g (i) g g l e d

5. The puppy chewed on Akiko's green slipper.
   c h e w (e) d

What is Akiko's puppy's name? Write the circled letters from your answers on the lines below to spell out the puppy's name.
   A n n i e

88

NAME_____

Lesson 1.4 Verbs

Complete It

Fill in each blank with a verb from the box. Some verbs can be used in more than one sentence.

ran	gave	played
took	threw	chased

1. Sam and Hailey ___took___ their dogs, Muffy and Baxter, to the park.

2. The dogs ___played___ in a pond.

3. They ___ran___ around the park again and again.

4. Hailey ___threw___ a stick.

5. Muffy and Baxter ___chased___ the stick.

6. Sam and Hailey ___gave___ Muffy and Baxter two big bones.

Try It

1. What else could Muffy and Baxter do at the park? Write another sentence. Circle the verb.
   Answers will vary.

2. What do you think Sam and Hailey will do when they get home from the park? Write a sentence. Circle the verb.
   Answers will vary.

89

Language Arts Grade 2 Answers

NAME

Lesson 1.5 Adjectives

Adjectives are words that describe. They give more information about nouns. Adjectives often answer the question **What kind?**

Kyle has a shirt.   Kyle has a **striped** shirt.

The adjective **striped** tells **what kind** of shirt Kyle has.

The adjectives in the sentences below are in bold.

Linh put the **yellow** flowers on the **wooden** table.
Jess has **curly**, **red** hair.
The **bright** moon shone in the **dark** sky.

Match It

Choose the adjective from the second column that best describes each noun in the first column. Write the letter of the adjective on the line. Some answers can be used twice.

1. the ___d___ sunshine   a. green
2. the ___c___ bird   b. rough
3. the ___a___ grass   c. chirping
4. the ___f___ squirrel   d. warm
5. the ___b___ bark of the tree   e. noisy
6. the ___e___ lawnmower   f. furry

| Tip | Adjectives do not always come before nouns: **The sky is blue**. The adjective **blue** describes the noun **sky**, but it does not come right before it in the sentence. |

90

NAME

Lesson 1.5 Adjectives

Identify It

Read the sentences below. Circle the adjectives. Then, underline the nouns the adjectives describe.

Example: Kirsten made some (cold)(sweet) lemonade.

1. A (large) raccoon lives in the woods near my house.
2. Raccoons have (four) legs and (bushy) tails.
3. They have (black) patches on their faces.
4. It looks like they are wearing (funny) masks.
5. Raccoons also have (dark) rings on their tails.
6. They sleep in (warm) dens in the winter.
7. Raccoons eat (fresh) fruit, eggs, and insects.

Try It

1. Write a sentence that describes an animal you have seen in the wild. Use two adjectives.

   Answers will vary.

2. Where do you think this animal lives? Write a sentence that describes the animal's home. Use two adjectives.

   Answers will vary.

91

NAME

Lesson 1.6 Adverbs

Adverbs are words that describe verbs. Adverbs often answer the questions **When?**, **Where?**, or **How?**

She **quickly** opened the umbrella.
Quickly tells **how** the umbrella was opened.

We will go to the museum **later**.
Later tells **when** we will go to the museum.

Maya ran **down** the street.
Down tells **where** Maya ran.

Identify It

Circle the adverb in each sentence below. Then, decide if the adverb tells **when**, **where**, or **how**. Write **when**, **where**, or **how** on the line beside the sentence.

1. (Yesterday,) it snowed. ___when___
2. Big flakes fell (gently) to the ground. ___how___
3. Ian looked (everywhere) for his mittens. ___where___
4. He (quickly) put on his boots and hat. ___how___
5. He opened the door and walked (outside) ___where___
6. Ian (quietly) listened to the snow falling. ___how___

| Tip | Adverbs often end with the letters **ly**. Here are some adverbs: **lightly, slowly, softly, evenly, joyfully,** and **loosely**. |

92

NAME

Lesson 1.6 Adverbs

Complete It

An adverb is missing from each sentence below. Choose the correct adverb from the words in parentheses ( ). Write it in the blank.

1. Ian ___quickly___ ran to his friend Ming's house. (quickly, quick)
2. He knocked ___loudly___ at the back door. (loud, loudly)
3. ___Soon___, Ming was ready to play in the snow. (Soon, Sooner)
4. Ming's brother, Jin, came home ___early___. (early, earliest)
5. He ___happily___ joined Ming and Ian in the yard. (happy, happily)
6. ___First___, they built a snowman. (First, Last)
7. Jin ___playfully___ tossed a snowball at his sister. (playful, playfully)
8. Ming, Jin, and Ian went ___inside___ for some hot cocoa. (inside, into)

Try It

Write a sentence that tells about something you did with your friends. Use at least one of these adverbs in your sentence: **slowly, quickly, loudly, quietly, easily, suddenly, before, later, after, sometimes**.

   Answers will vary.

| Tip | When you are looking for the adverb in a sentence, sometimes it helps to find the verb first. Then, ask yourself **When?**, **Where?**, or **How?** about the verb. |

93

Language Arts Grade 2 Answers

Lesson 1.7 Statements

A **statement** is a sentence that begins with a capital letter and ends with a period. A statement tells the reader something. Each of the following sentences is a statement.

My brother and I fly kites when we go to the beach.
My kite is shaped like a diamond.
It is purple, blue, and green.
It has a long tail.

Rewrite It

Rewrite the following sentences. Each statement should begin with a capital letter and end with a period.

1. people have flown kites for thousands of years

   People have flown kites for thousands of years.

2. some kites are shaped like dragons or fish

   Some kites are shaped like dragons or fish.

3. others are shaped like birds

   Others are shaped like birds.

4. flying kites is a fun hobby

   Flying kites is a fun hobby.

94

Lesson 1.7 Statements

Proof It

Read the following paragraphs. Each statement should begin with a capital letter and end with a period. Use this proofreading mark (≡) under a letter to make it a capital. Use this proofreading mark (⊙) to add a period.

Example: nick and Matt made a kite shaped like a frog⊙

    early kites were made in China. They were covered with silk. Other kites were covered with paper. the material covering the wooden sticks was sometimes painted by hand⊙

    benjamin Franklin did experiments with kites. Alexander Graham Bell also used kites in his experiments.

    today, kite festivals are held in many cities. people come from all around the world. They like to share their kites with other kite lovers. some kites are tiny. Others measure as much as one hundred feet⊙

Try It

1. What kind of kite would you make? Write a statement about it.

   Answers will vary.

2. Where would you fly the kite? Write a statement about it.

   Answers will vary.

95

Lesson 1.8 Questions

Questions are sentences that ask something. A question begins with a capital letter and ends with a question mark.

Where are your shoes?
Have you seen my hat?
Did you put my mittens away?

Proof It

Read the letter below. Find the four periods that should be question marks. Write question marks in their place.

Dear Taylor,
  How are you? I am having a great time on vacation. Have you ever been to Florida? I have never seen so many palm trees. Yesterday, we went to the ocean. Can you guess what I found on the beach? I found a jellyfish and sand dollar.
  We had a cookout with my cousins on Tuesday. I tried three kinds of fresh fish. Do you like fish? I like it more than I thought I would.
  That is all the news from Florida. I hope you are having a good vacation, too.

Your friend,

Isabel

Tip	Questions often begin with words like these: **who, what, when, where, why, how, did, do, will,** and **can.**

96

Lesson 1.8 Questions

Complete It

Read the sentences that follow. If a sentence is a statement, add a period on the line. If a sentence is a question, add a question mark on the line.

1. Isabel and her family drove to Florida .
2. Do you know how long it took them to get there ?
3. They drove for three days .
4. Isabel has two sisters .
5. What did the girls do during the long drive ?
6. Did they play games in the car ?
7. Everyone in Isabel's family likes to sing .
8. Where will they go on vacation next year ?

Try It

On the lines below, write two questions you could ask Isabel about her vacation. Make sure each question begins with a capital letter and ends with a question mark.

Answers will vary.

97

Language Arts Grade 2 Answers

NAME

Lesson 1.9 Exclamations

Exclamations are sentences that are said with great feeling. They show excitement or surprise. Exclamations begin with a capital letter and end with an exclamation point.

(T)anisha won the race(!)
(I) love your new jacket(!)
(T)here is something scary under the bed(!)

Rewrite It

Rewrite the following sentences. Each exclamation should begin with a capital letter and end with an exclamation point.

1. we won the game
   We won the game!

2. maggie hit six homeruns
   Maggie hit six homeruns!

3. she set a record
   She set a record!

4. we are the school champions
   We are the school champions!

| Tip | Some exclamations can be a single word. **Surprise! Hurray! Ouch! No!** |

98

NAME

Lesson 1.9 Exclamations

Proof It

Read the following diary entry. Find the six periods that should be exclamation points. Write exclamation points in their place.

Tuesday, April 7
Dear Diary,
   Today began like any other day. I had no idea what was in store for me, I brought the mail in the house. There was a blue envelope. Hurray, It was just what I had been waiting for. I opened it and pulled out the letter. Here is what it said: Congratulations, You are the grand-prize winner,
   I ran upstairs to find my mom. I could not wait to tell her the news. We had won a free vacation, I knew she would be amazed. I enter many contests. I do not usually win, though. What a great day,

Try It

Imagine that you are telling a friend about something exciting that happened to you. Write two sentences that are exclamations. Remember to begin with a capital letter and end with an exclamation point.

1. Answers will vary.

2. Answers will vary.

99

NAME

Lesson 1.10 Commands

Commands are sentences that tell you to do something. Commands begin with a capital letter. They end with a period.

(D)o not forget your lunch(.)   (R)ead the other book first(.)

(C)lose the door(.)   (L)ook inside the box(.)

Statements usually begin with a noun or a pronoun. Commands often begin with a verb. Look at the examples above. The words **do**, **read**, **close**, and **look** are all verbs.

Identify It

Read each sentence below. If it is a command, write **C** on the line. If it is a statement, write **S** on the line.

1. Tia and her grandpa like to bake together. S
2. They follow special rules in the kitchen. S
3. Wash your hands after you touch raw eggs. C
4. Be careful when the stove is hot. C
5. Read the recipe before you begin. C
6. Measure the ingredients. C
7. Tia makes tasty oatmeal cookies. S
8. Grandpa likes to make cornbread. S

100

NAME

Lesson 1.10 Commands

Complete It

Each of the following commands is missing a word and an end mark. Choose the word from the box that best completes each command. Then, add the correct end mark.

Drink	Chop	Put
Fill	Blend	Turn

How to Make a Berry Good Smoothie

1. Chop a banana into small pieces.
2. Put some berries and the banana pieces in the blender.
3. Fill the blender halfway with milk and orange juice.
4. Turn on the blender.
5. Blend the ingredients until they are smooth.
6. Drink the smoothie from a tall glass.

Try It

Think of two rules you need to follow at school. Write them as commands.

Example: Listen quietly when the teacher talks.

1. Answers will vary.
2. Answers will vary.

101

Language Arts Grade 2 Answers

NAME_____

Lesson 1.11 Combining Sentences (Nouns)

Sometimes, sentences can be combined.

> Bats eat bugs.   Frogs eat bugs.

Both sentences tell about things that eat insects. These two sentences can be combined into one by using the word **and**.

> Bats **and** frogs eat bugs.

Here is another example.

> Children like to go to the beach.
> Adults like to go to the beach.
> Children **and** adults like to go to the beach.

Identify It

Read each pair of sentences below. If the sentences can be joined with the word **and**, make a check mark (✓) on the line. If not, leave the line blank.

1. Blue jays visit my birdfeeder. Robins visit my birdfeeder. __✓__

2. Parrots live in warm places. Penguins live in cold places. ____

3. Hawks build nests on ledges. Eagles build nests on ledges. __✓__

4. Hummingbirds like flowers. Bees like flowers. __✓__

5. Geese fly south for the winter. Owls do not fly south in the winter.
   ____

102

NAME_____

Lesson 1.11 Combining Sentences (Nouns)

Rewrite It

Combine each pair of sentences below into one sentence. Write the new sentence.

1. Herons live near water. Mallards live near water.
   <u>Herons and mallards live near water.</u>

2. Sparrows are mostly brown. Wrens are mostly brown.
   <u>Sparrows and wrens are mostly brown.</u>

3. Cardinals eat seeds. Finches eat seeds.
   <u>Cardinals and finches eat seeds.</u>

4. Crows are completely black. Grackles are completely black.
   <u>Crows and grackles are completely black.</u>

Try It

1. Think of two things that are the same in some way. They might be the same color or the same size. They might eat the same thing or like doing the same thing. Write a pair of sentences about the two things you chose.

   Example: Cats like to be petted.   Dogs like to be petted.
   <u>Answers will vary.</u>

2. Now, combine the two sentences you wrote into one.
   <u>Answers will vary.</u>

103

NAME_____

Lesson 1.12 Combining Sentences (Verbs)

Sometimes sentences can be combined.
> Julia bikes on Saturday morning.
> Julia jogs on Saturday morning.

Both sentences tell what Julia does on Saturday morning. These two sentences can be joined using the word **and**.
> Julia bikes **and** jogs on Saturday morning.

Complete It

Read the sentences below. Fill in each space with the missing word or words.

1. Mom carried out the birthday cake. Mom placed it on the table.
   <u>Mom</u> carried out the birthday cake <u>and</u>
   placed it on the table.

2. Carmen took a deep breath. Carmen blew out the candles.
   <u>Carmen</u> took a deep breath <u>and</u> blew out the
   candles.

3. The children sang "Happy Birthday." The children clapped for Carmen.
   <u>The children</u> sang "Happy Birthday" <u>and</u>
   clapped for Carmen.

104

NAME_____

Lesson 1.12 Combining Sentences (Verbs)

Rewrite It

Combine each pair of sentences below into one sentence.

1. Carmen unwrapped her presents. Carmen opened the boxes.
   <u>Carmen unwrapped her presents and opened the boxes.</u>

2. Carmen smiled. Carmen thanked her friends for the gifts.
   <u>Carmen smiled and thanked her friends for the gifts.</u>

3. Everyone played freeze tag. Everyone had a good time.
   <u>Everyone played freeze tag and had a good time.</u>

4. The guests ate some cake. The guests drank pink lemonade.
   <u>The guests ate some cake and drank pink lemonade.</u>

Try It

1. Write two sentences that tell about things you do. Use a different verb in each sentence.

   Example: Carmen sings in a choir. Carmen plays the piano.
   <u>Answers will vary.</u>

2. Now, combine the two sentences you wrote using the word **and**.

   Example: Carmen sings in a choir and plays the piano.
   <u>Answers will vary.</u>

105

Language Arts Grade 2 Answers

NAME _____

Lesson 1.13 Combining Sentences (Adjectives)

Sometimes sentences can be combined.

The wagon was red.　　　The wagon was shiny.

The adjectives **red** and **shiny** both describe **wagon**. These two sentences can be combined into one by using the word **and**.

The wagon was red **and** shiny.

Here is another example.

Danny has a new scooter.　　　The scooter is blue.

The adjectives **new** and **blue** describe Danny's scooter. The two sentences can be combined.

Danny has a **new blue** scooter.

Identify It

Read each pair of sentences below. If the adjectives in both sentences describe the same person or thing, the sentences can be combined. Make a check mark (✓) on the line if the two sentences can be combined.

1. Oliver's painting is bright. Oliver's painting is cheerful. ✓

2. Oliver painted the flower garden. The garden was colorful. ✓

3. Oliver's paintbrush is soft. Oliver's paints are new. _____

4. The wall is large. The wall is white. ✓

5. The tulips are red. The rosebushes are big. _____

106

NAME _____

Lesson 1.13 Combining Sentences (Adjectives)

Rewrite It

Combine each pair of sentences below into one sentence.

1. The paints are shiny. The paints are wet.

The paints are shiny and wet.

2. The afternoon is warm. The afternoon is sunny.

The afternoon is warm and sunny.

3. Oliver's paintings are beautiful. Oliver's paintings are popular.

Oliver's paintings are beautiful and popular.

4. The red tulips are Oliver's favorite. The tulips are pretty.

The pretty red tulips are Oliver's favorite.

Try It

1. Write two sentences that describe your hair. Use a different adjective in each sentence.

Example: My hair is red.　　　My hair is curly.

Answers will vary.

2. Now write a sentence that combines the two sentences you wrote.

Example: My hair is red and curly.

Answers will vary.

107

Chapter 2　　　NAME _____

Lesson 2.1 Capitalizing the First Word in a Sentence

All sentences begin with a capital letter. A capital letter is a sign to the reader that a new sentence is starting.

Marisol colored the leaves with a green crayon.
Alexander loves to dance.

The bus will arrive at three o'clock.
Is the book on the coffee table?

I love your backpack!
Raise your left hand.

Proof It

Read the paragraphs below. The first word of every sentence should begin with a capital letter. To show that a letter should be a capital, underline it three times (≡). Then, write the capital letter above it.

Example: <u>y</u>our socks don't match.

　　T
<u>t</u>ree trunks can tell the story of a tree's life. <u>a</u> slice of a tree trunk shows many rings. <u>a</u> tree adds a new ring every year. <u>e</u>ach ring has a light part and a dark part. <u>w</u>hen scientists look at the rings, they learn about the tree.

　　T
<u>t</u>he rings can tell how old a tree is. <u>t</u>hey can tell what the weather was like. <u>i</u>f there was a fire or a flood, the rings will show it. <u>t</u>rees cannot talk, but they do tell stories.

108

NAME _____

Lesson 2.1 Capitalizing the First Word in a Sentence

Rewrite It

Rewrite each sentence below. Make sure your sentences begin with a capital letter.

1. the oldest living tree is in California.

The oldest living tree is in California.

2. it is located in the White Mountains.

It is located in the White Mountains.

3. the tree is more than 4,600 years old.

The tree is more than 4,600 years old.

4. scientists named the tree Methuselah.

Scientists named the tree Methuselah.

5. would you like to visit this tree one day?

Would you like to visit this tree one day?

Try It

1. Write a sentence about something very old. Be sure to start your sentence with a capital letter.

Answers will vary.

2. Write a sentence that explains one reason you like trees. Be sure to start your sentence with a capital letter.

Answers will vary.

109

Language Arts Grade 2 Answers

NAME_____

Lesson 2.2 Capitalizing Names

The **name of a person or a pet** always begins with a capital letter.

(J)asper is (E)mily's brother.

The baby polar bear's name is (A)rthur.

Mom always buys (S)niffy's tissues.

Complete It

Complete each sentence below. Write each name in parentheses ( ). Remember to capitalize the names of people, pets, and products.

1. <u>Cassie's</u> (cassie's) favorite food is corn on the cob.

2. <u>Omar</u> (omar) loves olives and oranges.

3. <u>Peter's</u> (peter's) pet parakeet, <u>Prudence</u> (prudence), eats <u>Pet Food Plus</u> (pet food plus) peanuts.

4. <u>Auntie Ann's Apple Crunch</u> (auntie ann's apple crunch) is <u>Amy's</u> (amy's) favorite cereal.

5. <u>Bradley's</u> (bradley's) bunny, <u>Boris</u> (boris), eats beets.

6. <u>Tess</u> (tess) and <u>Tom</u> (tom) like <u>Tito's Tasty Tacos</u> (tito's tasty tacos).

110

NAME_____

Lesson 2.2 Capitalizing Names

Proof It

Read the paragraph below. The names of people, pets, and products should begin with a capital letter. To show that a letter should be capital, underline it three times (≡). Then, write the capital letter above it.

The neighborhood was getting ready to have a pet show. Geoffrey and g̲i̲n̲a̲ brushed their pet gerbil, g̲e̲o̲r̲g̲e̲, with a groom-easy brush they bought at the pet store. h̲a̲n̲k̲ and h̲a̲r̲r̲y̲'s hamster, h̲i̲l̲d̲a̲, was ready to perform all her tricks. Sandeep tightly held his snake, s̲i̲m̲o̲n̲.

The show was ready to start. Only f̲r̲a̲n̲c̲e̲s̲ and her flamingo, Flora, were still missing. f̲r̲a̲n̲c̲e̲s̲ had to finish giving f̲l̲o̲r̲a̲ a bath with c̲l̲e̲a̲n̲ c̲r̲i̲t̲t̲e̲r̲s̲ shampoo. Finally, they arrived. The pet show could begin!

Try It

1. Write a sentence using the names of three of your friends.

<u>Answers will vary.</u>

2. Imagine you had one of the following pets: a hippo, a lion, a whale, a bear, or an anteater. Write a sentence about what you would name your pet.

<u>Answers will vary.</u>

111

NAME_____

Lesson 2.3 Capitalizing Titles

A **title** is a word that comes before a person's name. A title gives more information about who a person is. Titles that come before a name begin with a capital letter.

(G)randma Sheryl   (U)ncle David
(C)ousin Ella   (P)resident George Washington
(D)octor Wright   (J)udge Thomas

Titles of respect also begin with a capital letter. Here are some titles of respect: **Mr., Mrs., Ms.,** and **Miss.**

(M)r. Garza   (M)iss Sullivan   (M)s. Romano   (M)rs. Chun

Proof It

Read the diary entry below. All titles should begin with a capital letter. To show that a letter should be a capital, underline it three times (≡). Then, write the capital letter above it.

Dear Diary,

Last night, I went to a play with a̲unt Sonia and u̲ncle Pat. I sat next to c̲ousin Fiona and c̲ousin Nora. The play was about m̲s. Amelia Earhart, the first woman to fly across the Atlantic Ocean alone. m̲s. Earhart led an exciting life. She even met p̲resident Roosevelt.

After the play, I met Aunt Sonia's friend, m̲rs. Angley. She played the role of m̲s. Earhart. I also met m̲r. Roche. He played the role of p̲resident Roosevelt. He was very kind and funny.

112

NAME_____

Lesson 2.3 Capitalizing Titles

Rewrite It

Rewrite each of the following sentences. Remember, titles begin with a capital letter.

1. ms. Earhart lived an exciting life.
<u>Ms. Earhart lived an exciting life.</u>

2. Her husband, mr. George Putnam, printed a book about her last journey.
<u>Her husband, Mr. George Putnam, printed a book about her last journey.</u>

3. grandpa Leo gave aunt Sonia the book.
<u>Grandpa Leo gave Aunt Sonia the book.</u>

4. grandma Lucy read it last year.
<u>Grandma Lucy read it last year.</u>

5. She also read a book about mrs. Roosevelt.
<u>She also read a book about Mrs. Roosevelt.</u>

Try It

What person from history would you like to meet? Use the person's title in your answer.
<u>Answers will vary.</u>

113

Language Arts Grade 2 Answers

Lesson 2.4 Capitalizing Place Names

The **names of special places** always begin with a capital letter.

Ⓡockwell Ⓔlementary Ⓢchool   Ⓖarner Ⓢcience Ⓜuseum

Ⓞrlando, Ⓕlorida   Ⓑay Ⓥillage Ⓛibrary

Ⓜississippi Ⓡiver   Ⓜars

Ⓓonovan Ⓢtreet   Ⓕrance

Complete It

Complete each sentence below with the word in parentheses ( ). Remember, special places begin with a capital letter.

1. My family left Charlotte, __North Carolina__ (north carolina), yesterday morning.

2. We waved good-bye to our house on __Clancy Avenue__ (clancy avenue).

3. We passed __Washington Elementary School__ (washington elementary school).

4. Then, we crossed __Hilliard Bridge__ (hilliard bridge).

5. We were on our way across the __United States__ (united states)!

114

Lesson 2.4 Capitalizing Place Names

Proof It

Read the postcard below. Find the 15 words that should begin with a capital letter. Underline each letter that should be a capital three times (≡). Then, write the capital letter above it.

Hi Annie,
   I am writing from A̲rizona. Today, we went to the T̲ucson C̲hildren's M̲useum. Tomorrow, we will head to the grand C̲anyon. Next week, we'll be in C̲alifornia. We will visit S̲tanford U̲niversity. That is where my parents went to college. Then, we will head north. I can't wait to see redwood N̲ational F̲orest.
   Your pal,
   Priya

United States

Annie Schneider
452 C̲herry L̲ane
C̲harlotte, NC 22471

Try It

1. What state or city would you like to visit? Be sure to capitalize the name in your answer.

   __Answers will vary.__

2. What school do you go to? Write your answer on the line below. Use capital letters where they are needed.

   __Answers will vary.__

115

Lesson 2.5 Capitalizing Days, Months, and Holidays

The **days of the week** each begin with a capital letter.
Ⓜonday, Ⓣuesday, Ⓦednesday, Ⓣhursday, Ⓕriday, Ⓢaturday, Ⓢunday

The **months of the year** are also capitalized.
Ⓙanuary, Ⓜay, Ⓙune, Ⓞctober

The **names of holidays** begin with a capital letter.
Ⓒhristmas, Ⓣhanksgiving, Ⓥalentine's Ⓓay, Ⓚwanzaa

Proof It

Read the sentences below. Underline each letter that should be a capital three times (≡). Then, write the capital letter above it.

1. I have to go to the doctor on M̲onday.

2. Softball practice starts on T̲uesday afternoon.

3. W̲ednesday is Miguel's birthday.

4. There is no school on P̲residents' D̲ay.

5. I will go to my piano lesson on F̲riday.

6. We will go to the grocery store on S̲aturday morning.

7. Grandma will visit during H̲anukkah.

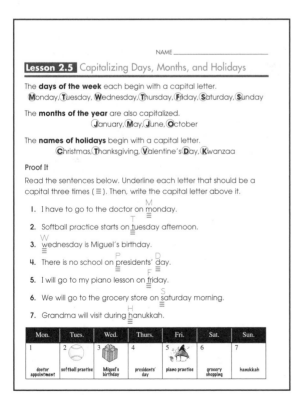

Mon.	Tues.	Wed.	Thurs.	Fri.	Sat.	Sun.
1 doctor appointment	2 softball practice	3 Miguel's birthday	4	5 presidents' day	6 grocery shopping	7 hanukkah

116

Lesson 2.5 Capitalizing Days, Months, and Holidays

Rewrite It

The Brandon family keeps a list of important holidays and dates. Read the list. If the date or holiday is written correctly, make a check mark (✓) on the line. If it is not written correctly, rewrite it.

Ella's birthday	january 20	January 20
valentine's Day	February 14	Valentine's Day
Shane's party	May 11	✓
Kahlil's first birthday	june 22	June 22
the Cheswicks' trip	july 18	July 18
thanksgiving	November 23	Thanksgiving
Tyson's birthday	december 29	December 29

Try It

1. Write a sentence about something that happened this week. Tell what day of the week it happened.

   __Answers will vary.__

2. What is your favorite holiday? Why?

   __Answers will vary.__

117

Language Arts Grade 2 Answers

NAME

Lesson 2.6 Periods

Periods are used at the ends of statements and commands. They tell the reader that a sentence has ended.

We ate tomato soup for lunch.
It will probably rain this afternoon.
Run as fast as you can.
Kris was wearing a blue baseball cap.

Proof It

Read the paragraph below. It is missing six periods. Add the missing periods. Circle each one so that it is easy to see.

Tip	A capital letter can be a sign that a new sentence is beginning.

Most people do not like mosquitoes.If you spend any time outside in the summer, you will probably get bitten.Not all mosquitoes bite people.Only female mosquitoes bite people.When mosquitoes bite, they take a drop of blood from a person.Some mosquitoes like birds or flowers better.

118

NAME

Lesson 2.6 Periods

Rewrite It

Rewrite the following sentences. Each one should end with a period. Circle the periods.

1. There are thousands of types of mosquitoes
There are thousands of types of mosquitoes.

2. Mosquitoes like human sweat
Mosquitoes like human sweat.

3. Some people never get mosquito bites
Some people never get mosquito bites.

4. Mosquitoes lay eggs in still water
Mosquitoes lay eggs in still water.

5. Bug spray can protect you from bites
Bug spray can protect you from bites.

Try It

Have you ever been bitten by a bug? Write two sentences about it. Both sentences should end with a period.

Answers will vary.

119

NAME

Lesson 2.7 Question Marks

Use a **question mark** to end a sentence that asks a question.

Where did you put the crayons**?**
What time will Grandpa get here**?**
How did you like the play**?**
Did you go swimming**?**

Complete It

Read each answer below. Then, write the question that goes with the answer.

Example: **Q:** What color is the sweater?
A: The sweater is yellow.

1. **Q:** What did you eat for dinner?
A: I ate spaghetti for dinner.

2. **Q:** Where is your skateboard?
A: My skateboard is in the garage.

3. **Q:** Where did Keiko go?
A: Keiko went to the library.

4. **Q:** How old is Ashton?
A: Ashton is seven years old.

5. **Q:** Where does Mr. Arnold live?
A: Mr. Arnold lives in Houston.

6. **Q:** What is the book about?
A: The book is about a boy who wishes he could fly.

120

NAME

Lesson 2.7 Question Marks

Proof It

Theo is asking an author questions for a school report. Cross out the six wrong end marks. Add the correct end marks, and circle them.

Theo: What do you like about being a writer**?**

Ms. Loden: I love to tell stories.

Theo: Where do you get your ideas**?**

Ms. Loden: I used to be a teacher. Many ideas come from the children who were in my classes.

Theo: When do you write**?**

Ms. Loden: I write for about four hours every morning.

Theo: Do you have any hobbies**?**

Ms. Loden: I like to garden, ski, and do crossword puzzles.

Try It

What are two questions you would like to ask the author of your favorite book? Write them on the lines below. Remember to end each question with a question mark.

Answers will vary.

121

Language Arts Grade 2 Answers

Lesson 2.8 Exclamation Points

An **exclamation point** is used to end a sentence that is exciting. Sometimes exclamation points are used to show surprise.

Look at the rainbow!   I loved that movie!

Wow!   My class got a new computer!

Proof It

Read the poster below. Six exclamation points and two periods are missing. Add the end marks where they are needed.

Hurray!

THE BELLVIEW FAIR

is coming to town in July!

Win great prizes!

Ride the biggest Ferris wheel
in Clark County!

Sample tasty foods
from around the world!

Admission is $3.00 for adults
and $2.00 for kids under twelve.

The fair opens July 6 and closes July 12.

DON'T MISS ALL THE FUN!

122

Lesson 2.8 Exclamation Points

Complete It

Read the sentences below. One sentence in each pair should end with a period. One should end with an exclamation point. Add the correct end marks.

1. I went to the Bellview Fair.
   I had the best time!

2. I played a game called Toss the Ring.
   I won four stuffed animals!

3. All the sheep escaped from their pen!
   It did not take the farmers long to catch them, though.

4. I ate a snow cone and some cotton candy.
   The cotton candy got stuck in my hair!

Try It

Think about an exciting place you have been. It could be a fair, sports event, field trip, or vacation. Write two exciting things that happened. End each sentence with an exclamation point.

Example: Yea, he hit a homerun! Wow, what a game!

Answers will vary.

123

Lesson 2.9 Periods in Abbreviations

An **abbreviation** is a short way of writing something. Most abbreviations are followed by a period.

The **days of the week** can be abbreviated.
Mon. Tues. Wed. Thurs. Fri. Sat. Sun.

The **months of the year** also can be abbreviated. **May**, **June**, and **July** are not abbreviated because their names are so short.
Jan. Feb. Mar. Apr. Aug. Sept. Oct. Nov. Dec.

People's titles are almost always abbreviated when they come before a name.
Mrs. = mistress Mr. = mister Dr. = doctor

Types of streets are abbreviated in addresses.
St. = street Ave. = avenue Dr. = drive Ln. = lane

Match It

Read each underlined word in the first column. Find the matching abbreviation in the second column. Write the letter of the abbreviation on the line.

1. __e__ 19052 Inglewood <u>Avenue</u>   **a.** Thurs.

2. __c__ <u>Doctor</u> Weinstein   **b.** Jan.

3. __a__ <u>Thursday</u> night   **c.** Dr.

4. __f__ <u>October</u> 15, 2006   **d.** Ln.

5. __d__ 18 Winding Creek <u>Lane</u>   **e.** Ave.

6. __b__ <u>January</u> 1, 2000   **f.** Oct.

124

Lesson 2.9 Periods in Abbreviations

Complete It

Read each word in parentheses ( ). Write the abbreviation.

Example: Sunday, ___Nov.___ (November) 12

1. 4250 Rosehill ___St.___ (Street)

2. ___Mr.___ (Mister) Ortega

3. ___Apr.___ (April) 4, 2014

4. ___Feb.___ (February) 10, 1904

5. ___Wed.___ (Wednesday) morning

6. ___Mrs.___ (Mistress) Antonivic

7. Beech ___Dr.___ (Drive)

February

Try It

1. Write your street address or school address using an abbreviation. Here are some other abbreviations you may need:

   Rd. = road   Blvd. = boulevard   Ct. = court   Cir. = circle

   Answers will vary.

2. Write today's date using an abbreviation for the day of the week and month.

   Answers will vary.

125

Language Arts Grade 2 Answers

Lesson 2.10 Commas with Dates, Cities, and States

Commas are used in dates. They are used in between the day of the month and the year.

January 1 1, 1988   October 8, 1845   June 25, 2015

Commas are also used in between the names of cities and states.

Charleston, South Carolina   Bangor, Maine

When the names of cities and states are in the middle of a sentence, a comma goes after the name of the state, too.

After we left Council Bluffs, Iowa, we headed north.
Meghan and Becca moved from Oxford, Ohio, to San Antonio, Texas.

Proof It

Read the words below. Eight commas are missing. Add each comma where it belongs by using this symbol (∧).

Example: Once you pass Huntsville, Alabama, you will be halfway there.

1. Selma was born on August 16, 2008.

2. She lives in Taos, New Mexico.

3. Her little sister was born on April 4, 2012.

4. Selma's grandparents live in Denver, Colorado.

5. It is a long drive from Denver, Colorado, to Taos, New Mexico.

6. The last time Selma's grandparents visited was December 20, 2013.

126

Lesson 2.10 Commas with Dates, Cities, and States

Identify It

Read each line below. If it is correct, make a check mark (✓) on the line. If it is wrong, rewrite it.

1. March, 4 1952 _March 4, 1952_

2. Butte Montana _Butte, Montana_

3. May 27 2001 _May 27, 2001_

4. The plane stopped in Baltimore, Maryland, to get more fuel.
   ✓

5. It snowed eight inches in Stowe Vermont.
   It snowed eight inches in Stowe, Vermont.

6. November 4, 2015 ✓

7. Gum Spring, Virginia is where my grandma lives.
   Gum Spring, Virginia, is where my

Try It _grandma lives._

1. Write a sentence about a city and state you would like to visit. Remember to use commas where they are needed.
   Answers will vary.

2. Ask a classmate when he or she was born. Write the date, including the year, on the line below.
   Answers will vary.

127

Lesson 2.11 Commas in Series and in Letters

A **series** is a list of words. Use a comma after each word in the series except the last word.

Mom bought carrots, lettuce, tomatoes, and peppers.
Cody's sisters are named Cassidy, Cameron, Casey, and Colleen.

In a letter, a comma follows **the greeting** and **the closing**.

Dear Mr. Wong,   Your friend,

Rewrite It

Rewrite the sentences below. Add commas to each list to make the sentences clearer.

1. Mom got out the picnic basket the plates and the cups.
   Mom got out the picnic basket, the plates,
   and the cups.

2. Lily packed forks knives spoons and napkins.
   Lily packed forks, knives, spoons, and
   napkins.

3. Amelia added pears oranges and apples.
   Amelia added pears, oranges, and apples.

4. Dad made sandwiches a salad and brownies.
   Dad made sandwiches, a salad, and
   brownies.

128

Lesson 2.11 Commas in Series and in Letters

Proof It

Read the letter below. Ten commas are missing. Add each comma where it belongs by using this symbol (∧).

Dear Grandma,

Yesterday, we went to the park. Lily, Amelia, and Mom shook out the picnic blanket. Dad carried the basket, the drinks, and the toys from the car. We all ate some salad, a sandwich, and a fruit.

Deepak, Sita, and Raj were at the park with their parents, too. We played tag and fed the ducks. Later, we shared our brownies with the Nair family. I wish you could have been there!

Love,

Max

Try It

1. Imagine you were going on a picnic. What three things would you bring with you? Remember to separate the things in your list with commas.
   Answers will vary.

2. Name three people who live on your street or go to your school. Separate their names with commas.
   Answers will vary.

129

Language Arts Grade 2 Answers

Lesson 2.12 Commas in Compound Sentences

A **compound sentence** is made up of two smaller sentences. The smaller sentences are joined by a comma and the word **and** or **but**.

Michelle went to the store.　She bought some markers.
Michelle went to the store, **and** she bought some markers.

Bats sleep during the day.　They are active at night.
Bats sleep during the day, **but** they are active at night.

Rewrite It

Read the sentences below. Combine them using a comma and the word **and** or **but**.

1. Abby rode her bike. Gilbert rode his scooter.
   Abby rode her bike, and Gilbert rode his scooter.

2. My new bedroom is big. My old bedroom was cozy.
   My new bedroom is big, but my old bedroom was cozy.

3. The black cat is beautiful. The orange cat is friendly.
   The black cat is beautiful, and the orange cat is friendly.

4. Roberto is quick. Sophie is more graceful.
   Roberto is quick, but Sophie is more graceful.

130

Lesson 2.12 Commas in Compound Sentences

Proof It

Read the paragraph below. Four commas are missing from compound sentences. Add each comma where it belongs by using this symbol (∧).

Tip Look for the words **and** or **but**. Ask yourself if they join two complete sentences.

The leaves of the poison ivy plant are shaped like almonds, and they come in groups of three. Poison ivy can cause a rash, and it can make you itch. The leaves of the plant contain oil that causes the rash. Some people can touch the plant, but they will not get a rash.

The oil can stick to your clothes. Washing with soap and water can get rid of the oil, and it can keep the rash from spreading.

Try It

Write a compound sentence about what you like to do and what a friend of yours likes to do. Remember to join the two parts of your sentence with a comma and the word **and** or **but**.

Example: I like to play at the park, and Deena likes to go swimming.
Answers will vary.

131

Lesson 2.13 Apostrophes in Possessives

When something belongs to a person or thing, they own it. An apostrophe and the letter **s** (**'s**) at the end of a word show that the person or thing is the owner.

the car**'s** engine　　　Stacy**'s** eyes

Jake**'s** laugh　　　the table**'s** leg

Rewrite It

Read each phrase below. Then, rewrite it on the line as a possessive.

Example: the coat of Kayla　　Kayla's coat

1. the roar of the lion　the lion's roar

2. the spots of the leopard　the leopard's spots

3. the trip of Amy　Amy's trip

4. the lens of the camera　the camera's lens

5. the hat of Tim　Tim's hat

6. the roof of the jeep　the jeep's roof

132

Lesson 2.13 Apostrophes in Possessives

Match It

Read the words below. Then, read the answer choices. Write the letter of your answer on the line.

1. __a__ the horn of the rhino
   a. the rhino's horn　　　**b.** the horn's rhino

2. __b__ the animals of Africa
   a. the animal's of Africa　　　**b.** Africa's animals

3. __b__ the photos of John
   a. John photo's　　　**b.** John's photos

4. __a__ the leader of the safari
   a. the safari's leader　　　**b.** the leader safari's

5. __b__ the favorite animal of Don
   a. Don's favorite animal's　　　**b.** Don's favorite animal

6. __b__ the baby of the hippo
   a. the baby's hippo　　　**b.** the hippo's baby

7. __a__ the tent of Sarah
   a. Sarah's tent　　　**b.** Sarah tent

Try It

1. On the line below, write something you like about one of your friends. Use the possessive form of your friend's name.

   Example: I like William's smile.
   Answers will vary.

133

Language Arts Grade 2 Answers

NAME

Lesson 2.14 Quotation Marks in Dialogue

Quotation marks are used around the exact words a person says. One set of quotation marks is used before the first word the person says. Another set is used at the end of the person's words.

> Jamal said, **"**I am going to play in a piano recital on Saturday.**"**
> **"**Do you like fresh apple pie?**"** asked the baker.
> **"**Hurray!**"** shouted Sydney. **"**Today is a snow day!**"**

Remember to put the second pair of quotation marks after the punctuation mark that ends the sentence.

Complete It

Read each sentence below. Underline the speaker's exact words. Then, add a set of quotation marks before and after the speaker's words.

Example: Enzo shouted, "Catch the ball, Katie!"

1. "Would you like to go to skiing this afternoon?" asked Mom.

2. Alyssa asked, "Where will we go?"

3. Mom said, "Wintergreen Mountain is not too far away."

4. "Can I bring a friend?" asked Zane.

5. Mom said, "You can each bring along one friend."

6. Alyssa said, "Riley will be so excited!"

> **Tip** The exact words people say are sometimes called **dialogue**. Quotation marks are used to show which words are dialogue.

134

NAME

Lesson 2.14 Quotation Marks in Dialogue

Rewrite It

Read each sentence below. Write the sentence again. Add quotation marks where they are needed. Remember to find the speaker's exact words first.

1. Have you ever been skiing? Zane asked his friend.
   "Have you ever been skiing?" Zane asked his friend.

2. Joey said, No, but it sounds like fun.
   Joey said, "No, but it sounds like fun."

3. Riley said, My grandpa taught me how to ski.
   Riley said, "My grandpa taught me how to ski."

4. She added, He lives near the mountains in Vermont.
   She added, "He lives near the mountains in Vermont."

Try It

Write two sentences that have people speaking. Begin each sentence with one of these phrases.

My mom said, My friend said, My sister said, My grandpa said,

1. Answers will vary.
2. Answers will vary.

135

NAME

Lesson 2.15 Titles of Books and Movies

The **titles of books and movies** are underlined in text. This lets the reader know that the underlined words are part of a title.

> Cristina's favorite movie is Because of Winn-Dixie.
> Harry wrote a book report on Nate the Great and the Musical Note.
> Roald Dahl is the author of James and the Giant Peach.
> I have seen the movie Aladdin four times.

Rewrite It

Read the sentences below. Rewrite each sentence and underline the title of each movie.

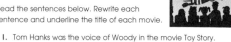

1. Tom Hanks was the voice of Woody in the movie Toy Story.
   Tom Hanks was the voice of Woody in the movie Toy Story.

2. Mara Wilson played Matilda Wormwood in the movie Matilda.
   Mara Wilson played Matilda Wormwood in the movie Matilda.

3. In the movie Shrek, Cameron Diaz was the voice of Princess Fiona.
   In the movie Shrek, Cameron Diaz was the voice of Princess Fiona.

4. The movie Fly Away Home is based on a true story.
   The movie Fly Away Home is based on a true story.

5. Harriet the Spy is the name of a book and a movie.
   Harriet the Spy is the name of a book and a movie.

136

NAME

Lesson 2.15 Titles of Books and Movies

Proof It

Read the paragraphs below. Find the five book titles and underline them.

Jon Scieszka (say **shez ka**) is a popular author. He has written many books for children. He is best known for his book The Stinky Cheese Man and Other Fairly Stupid Tales. Jon has always loved books. Dr. Seuss's famous book Green Eggs and Ham made Jon feel like he could be a writer one day.

In 1989, Jon wrote The True Story of the Three Little Pigs. Many children think his books are very funny. They also like the pictures. Lane Smith draws the pictures for many of Jon's books. They worked together on the book Math Curse. Their book Science Verse is also popular.

Try It

1. Write the title of your favorite book on the line below. Remember to underline it.
   Answers will vary.

2. What was the last movie you saw? Write the title on the line below. Remember to underline it.
   Answers will vary.

137

Language Arts Grade 2 Answers

Chapter 3
Lesson 3.1 Subject-Verb Agreement (Adding s)

NAME_____

When there is only one person or thing, add **s** to the end of an action verb.

> <u>Caleb</u> run**s** to the park.   <u>Ms. Wheeler</u> read**s** to us every day.

An action verb does not end with **s** when there is more than one person or thing, or when using **you**.

> <u>The balloons</u> float through the air.   <u>You</u> pull the string.

Complete It

Read each sentence below. Then, read the pair of verbs in parentheses ( ). Choose the correct verb form. Write it on the line.

1. Wade _____picks_____ a game for the family. (pick, picks)
2. He _____spins_____ the wheel. (spin, spins)
3. Wade _____draws_____ a picture on a big sheet of paper. (draw, draws)
4. Mom and Dad _____laugh_____. (laugh, laughs)
5. Alicia _____knows_____ what the picture is. (know, knows)
6. She _____rings_____ the bell. (ring, rings)
7. Alicia and Wade _____make_____ a good team. (make, makes)

138

Lesson 3.1 Subject-Verb Agreement (Adding s)

NAME_____

Proof It

Read each sentence below. Add an **s** to the end of the verb if needed.

1. The Andersons love__ game night.
2. Alicia choose_S_ the game.
3. She pick_S_ her favorite board game.
4. Mom, Dad, Alicia, and Wade roll__ the dice.
5. Wade take_S_ the first turn.
6. He move_S_ his piece four spaces.
7. Mom roll_S_ the dice.
8. Uh-oh! Mom lose_S_ her turn.
9. Mom never win_S_ this game!

Try It

Use a pair of verbs from the box to write two sentences. One sentence should have only one person or thing. The other sentence should have more than one person or thing.

run, runs	play, plays
smile, smiles	throw, throws

1. _Answers will vary._
2. _Answers will vary._

139

Lesson 3.2 Subject-Verb Agreement (Adding es)

NAME_____

Sometimes, **es** needs to be added instead of just **s**. Add **es** to verbs that end in **sh**, **ch**, **s**, **x**, and **z**.

> <u>Ellie</u> brush**es** her hair before she goes to bed.

> <u>Grandma</u> stitch**es** the letters on the pillow.

> <u>He</u> miss**es** his old house.

When there is more than one person or thing, verbs do not end in **s** or **es**.

Complete It

Read the sentences below. Choose the correct verb at the end of each sentence. Write it on the blank.

1. The bee _____buzzes_____ when it flies close to my ear. (buzz, buzzes)
2. Alexandra and Thomas _____wash_____ all the dishes after dinner. (wash, washes)
3. Manuel _____tosses_____ the ball to Ashley. (toss, tosses)
4. Noelle _____wishes_____ for something special when she blows out her candles. (wish, wishes)
5. Liam _____mixes_____ the batter before he pours it in the pan. (mix, mixes)

140

Lesson 3.2 Subject-Verb Agreement (Adding es)

NAME_____

Solve It

Circle the verb in each sentence below. If it is correct, make a check mark (✓) on the line. If it is not correct, write the correct form. Then, see if you can find each verb in the word search puzzle. Circle the verbs you find in the puzzle. Words can be found across and down.

1. Mom and Dad (relaxes) on the weekends. _relax_
2. The snake (hisses) at the bird. _____
3. Liza (catch) the bus each morning. _catches_
4. Sean (waxes) his surfboard on the beach. __✓__
5. The red sports car (pass) the truck. _____passes_____

r	e	l	a	x	o	h	k
w	d	j	u	t	c	i	q
a	p	a	s	s	e	s	c
x	g	j	b	b	o	s	w
e	c	a	t	c	h	e	s
s	e	h	k	u	l	s	y

Try It

Write two sentences. Correctly use a verb from the box in each sentence.

touch	misses
fixes	push
rush	crashes

1. _Answers will vary._

2. _Answers will vary._

141

Language Arts Grade 2 Answers

NAME _____

Lesson 3.3 Irregular Verbs: **Am**, **Is**, **Are**

Some verbs to do not show action. The verb **to be** does not show action. **Am**, **is**, and **are** are all different forms of the verb **to be**.

Am is used only with **I**.

    I **am** happy.   I **am** behind the door.

Is is used when there is only one person or thing.

    Tommy **is** my brother.   The sky **is** blue.

Are is used with **you**.

    You **are** lucky.   You **are** my friend.

Are is also used when there is more than one person or thing.

    Blanca and Charley **are** at school.   They **are** in second grade.

Complete It

Read each sentence below. Choose the correct verb from the parentheses ( ). Write it on the line.

1. I ___am___ tall and strong. (is, am)

2. You ___are___ a great cook. (are, am)

3. Gavin and Mitch ___are___ twins. (is, are)

4. This soup ___is___ too spicy! (is, am)

5. I ___am___ a niece. (are, am)

6. All the girls in my class ___are___ excited. (is, are)

7. That skateboard ___is___ broken. (are, is)

142

NAME _____

Lesson 3.3 Irregular Verbs: **Am**, **Is**, **Are**

Proof It

Read the diary entry below. The wrong forms of the verbs **am**, **is**, and **are** are used. Cross out each incorrect verb in bold type. Then, write the correct form above it.

> Thursday, May 27
>
> Dear Diary,
>
>   Victoria ~~are~~ *is* my friend. She knows lots of jokes. Today, I told
>
> her, "You ~~am~~ *are* the funniest person I know! I ~~are~~ *am* glad to be your
>
> friend."
>
>   We ~~is~~ *are* in a club together. Owen and Rachel ~~is~~ *are* in the club, too.
>
> We learn all kinds of jokes. Knock-knock jokes ~~is~~ *are* my favorite.
>
> Riddles ~~am~~ *are* Victoria's favorite.
>
>   Owen ~~is~~ older than us. He ~~am~~ *is* in third grade. He tells us all
>
> the third-grade jokes. We spend a lot of time laughing!

Try It

1. Write a sentence with only one person or thing. Use **is**.

    Answers will vary.

2. Write a sentence with more than one person or thing. Use **are**.

    Answers will vary.

143

NAME _____

Lesson 3.4 Irregular Verbs: **Has**, **Have**

Some verbs do not show action. The verb **to have** does not show action. **Has** and **have** are different forms of the verb **to have**.

Have is used with **I** or **you**.

    I **have** six cats.   You **have** a bird.

Have is also used when there is more than one person or thing.

    We **have** a French lesson this afternoon.

    They **have** a green car.

    Maureen and Ramon **have** brown hair.

    The tree and the plant **have** leaves.

Has is used when there is only one person or thing.

    She **has** two braids.   Lex **has** a book about fossils.

    The moon **has** a rough surface.

Complete It

Read each sentence below. Then, read the pair of verbs in parentheses. Choose the correct verb form and write it on the line.

1. Maple trees and oak trees ___have___ similar leaves. (has, have)

2. A gingko tree ___has___ leaves that look like fans. (has, have)

3. We ___have___ a large fir tree in the backyard. (has, have)

4. The Maddens ___have___ many trees that bloom in the spring. (has, have)

5. Lila ___has___ an enormous, old maple tree in the front yard. (has, have)

144

NAME _____

Lesson 3.4 Irregular Verbs: **Has**, **Have**

Proof It

There is a mistake with the verb in each sentence below. Cross out the incorrect verb. Then, write the correct verb above it.

1. Holly trees ~~has~~ *have* shiny red berries.

2. You ~~has~~ *have* a beautiful weeping willow tree.

3. An apple tree ~~have~~ *has* plenty of fruit in autumn.

4. A mulberry tree ~~have~~ *has* berries that birds love to eat.

5. Jaya and Chad ~~has~~ *have* a swing in the old oak tree.

6. I ~~has~~ *have* a piece of bark from the white birch tree.

7. Sparrows and chickadees ~~has~~ *have* a nest in the elm tree.

Try It

1. Write a sentence about something you have.

    Answers will vary.

2. Write a sentence about something one of your friends has.

    Answers will vary.

145

Language Arts Grade 2 Answers

Lesson 3.5 Forming the Past Tense by Adding **ed**

Verbs in the **present tense** tell about things that are happening right now. Verbs in the **past tense** tell about things that already happened. Add **ed** to most verbs to tell about the past.

Teresa jump**ed** over the log.   Grandma push**ed** the stroller.
The tall boy kick**ed** the ball.   Mr. Tisdall talk**ed** to the class.

If the verb already ends in **e**, just add **d**.
The family hik**ed** two miles. (hik**e**)
She plac**ed** the cups on the table. (plac**e**)

Complete It

The sentences below are missing verbs. Complete each sentence with the past tense of the verb in parentheses ( ).

1. Annie Smith Peck __traveled__ to many countries. (travel)

2. In 1888, she __climbed__ Mount Shasta in California. (climb)

3. She __hoped__ to climb the Matterhorn one day. (hope)

4. Annie __started__ a group called the American Alpine Club. (start)

5. She __explored__ the volcanoes of South America. (explore)

6. She __worked__ hard so she could climb in her spare time. (work)

7. Annie __continued__ climbing until she was 82. (continue)

146

Lesson 3.5 Forming the Past Tense by Adding **ed**

Rewrite It

Rewrite the sentences below in the past tense by adding ed to the underlined verb. If the verb already ends in **e**, just add **d** to change it to the past tense.

Example: Darby <u>pull</u> on his leash.   Darby **pulled** on his leash.

1. Annie Smith Peck <u>climb</u> many mountains.
   Annie Smith Peck climbed many mountains.

2. She <u>live</u> from 1850 until 1935.
   She lived from 1850 until 1935.

3. Annie <u>show</u> the world how strong women can be.
   Annie showed the world how strong women can be.

4. She <u>want</u> to set records in climbing.
   She wanted to set records in climbing.

Try It

Write two sentences about what you did last week. Make sure the verbs are in the past tense.

1. _____

2. _____

Answers will vary but should be written in the past tense.

147

Lesson 3.6 Past-Tense Verbs: **Was, Were**

The past tense of **am** and **is** is **was**. Remember to use **was** only if there is one person or thing.

I **was** tired.   The house **was** white.

The past tense of **are** is **were**. Remember to use **were** if there is more than one person or thing.

We **were** a team.   The monkeys **were** funny.

Complete It

Write the correct past-tense verb in the blanks below. Use **was** or **were**.

Last Tuesday, my brother Benjamin __was__ on TV. He __was__ at the park with his friend Allison. It __was__ a sunny day. They __were__ on the jungle gym. A news reporter __was__ at the park, too. She __was__ a reporter for Channel WBVA news. She asked people in the park if the city should build a new pool. Benjamin and Allison __were__ excited about the interview. My family watched Benjamin on the evening news. I __was__ proud of my brother, the TV star!

148

Lesson 3.6 Past-Tense Verbs: **Was, Were**

Rewrite It

The sentences below are in the present tense. Rewrite them in the past tense.

Example: The basketball <u>is</u> in the gym.   The basketball was in the gym.

1. Benjamin <u>is</u> worried we would miss the news.
   Benjamin was worried we would miss the news.

2. Mom and Dad <u>are</u> happy to see Ben's good manners.
   Mom and Dad were happy to see Ben's good manners.

3. I <u>am</u> glad Ben wore the hat I gave him.
   I was glad Ben wore the hat I gave him.

4. You <u>are</u> on vacation.
   You were on vacation.

Try It

1. Write a sentence about something that is happening right now. Use the verb **is** in your sentence.
   Answers will vary.

2. Now, write the same sentence in the past tense.
   Answers will vary.

149

Language Arts Grade 2 Answers

NAME _____

Lesson 3.7 Past-Tense Verbs: **Had**

The past tense of **have** and **has** is **had**.

Present Tense	Past Tense
I **have** four pets.	I **had** four pets.
The flowers **have** red petals.	The flowers **had** red petals.
Hayden **has** short hair.	Hayden **had** short hair.

Complete It

Complete each sentence with the correct form of the verb **have**. The word in parentheses ( ) will tell you to use the present tense or the past tense.

1. My bike ___has___ a horn and a scoop seat. (present)

2. My mom ___had___ a bike just like it when she was little. (past)

3. The wheels ___have___ shiny silver spokes. (present)

4. My mom's old bike ___had___ a bell, too. (past)

150

NAME _____

Lesson 3.7 Past-Tense Verbs: **Had**

Identify It

Read each sentence below. Circle the verb. If the sentence is in the present tense, write **pres**. in the space. If it is in the past tense, write **past**.

1. __pres.__ The one-dollar bill (has) a picture of George Washington on it.

2. __past__ I (had) our dollars in my piggybank.

3. __pres.__ The twenty-dollar bill (has) a picture of Andrew Jackson on it.

4. __past__ Greg and Dev (had) ten dollars to spend at the bookstore.

5. __pres.__ My sister (has) eight dollars.

6. __pres.__ My parents (have) a can collection.

7. __past__ Ian (had) a two-dollar bill.

Try It

1. Write a sentence about something you have.
   __Answers will vary.__

2. Now, rewrite your sentence in the past tense.
   __Answers will vary.__

151

NAME _____

Lesson 3.8 Past-Tense Verbs: **Went**

The past tense of the verb **go** is **went**.

Present Tense	Past Tense
We **go** to the fair with our cousins.	We **went** to the fair with our cousins.
Lorenzo **goes** to Florida.	Lorenzo **went** to Florida.

Rewrite It

Rewrite each sentence in the past tense.

1. We go to the store.
   __We went to the store.__

2. Trish goes to her singing lesson on Thursday.
   __Trish went to her singing lesson on Thursday.__

3. Sanjay goes home at noon.
   __Sanjay went home at noon.__

4. We go sledding with Miki and Ted.
   __We went sledding with Miki and Ted.__

152

NAME _____

Lesson 3.8 Past-Tense Verbs: **Went**

Proof It

Some of the verbs below are in the wrong tense. Cross out the underlined verbs. Write the correct past-tense verbs above them.

When my dad was little, his family ~~goes~~ *went* to a cabin every summer. He loved the little cabin in the woods, His cousins came to visit. Everyone ~~goes~~ *went* swimming in the lake. They ~~go~~ *went* on long bike rides. They built forts in the woods. Grandma and Grandpa ~~go~~ *went* for long walks. Once the entire family came from miles away. They ~~go~~ *went* to a big family party on the beach.

Dad loved those summers in the woods. Some day, he will take us to see the old cabin.

Try It

1. Write a sentence using the verb **go** or **goes**.
   __Answers will vary.__

2. Now, rewrite your sentence in the past tense.
   __Answers will vary.__

153

Language Arts Grade 2 Answers

Lesson 3.9 Past-Tense Verbs: **Saw**

The past tense of the verb **see** is **saw**.

Present Tense	Past Tense
My mom **sees** me swimming.	My mom **saw** me swimming.
Franco and Ana **see** the puppy every day.	Franco and Ana **saw** the puppy every day.

Rewrite It

Rewrite each sentence in the past tense.

1. We see raindrops on the leaves.
   We saw raindrops on the leaves.

2. The dragon sees the little girl climbing the hill.
   The dragon saw the little girl climbing the hill.

3. Dad sees the tiny cut when he put on his glasses.
   Dad saw the tiny cut when he put on his glasses.

4. The three birds see their mother.
   The three birds saw their mother.

5. Tess sees that movie three times.
   Tess saw that movie three times.

6. Cameron and Dillon see the hot air balloon.
   Cameron and Dillon saw the hot air balloon.

154

Lesson 3.9 Past-Tense Verbs: **Saw**

Proof It

Some of the verbs below are in the wrong tense. Cross out the underlined verbs. Write the correct past-tense verbs above them.

My aunt got married in Key West, Florida. We ~~see~~ saw many interesting things on our visit. My sister ~~sees~~ saw dolphins playing in the water. Dad took us to Ripley's Believe It or Not Museum. We ~~see~~ saw many strange and amazing things there. Later, we went to the Chicken Store. It is a place that rescues chickens. We ~~see~~ saw dozens of chickens there. I did not know Key West had so many homeless chickens!

Try It

1. What is the first thing you see when you wake up in the morning? Write your answer in the past tense.
   Answers will vary.

2. What is the first thing you see when you go to school? Write your answer in the past tense.
   Answers will vary.

155

Lesson 3.10 Contractions with **Not**

A **contraction** is a short way of saying something. In a contraction, two words are joined. An apostrophe (') goes in place of the missing letters.

Many contractions are formed with the word **not**. The apostrophe takes the place of the letter **o** in **not**.

is not = isn't	are not = aren't
was not = wasn't	were not = weren't
does not = doesn't	did not = didn't
have not = haven't	can not = can't

Match It

Match each pair of underlined words with its contraction. Write the letter of the contraction in the space.

1. _e_ The cat and the mouse are not friends.   **a.** can't
2. _a_ They can not get along.   **b.** isn't
3. _f_ They have not tried very hard, though.   **c.** wasn't
4. _c_ The cat was not friendly to the mouse.   **d.** weren't
5. _b_ The mouse is not kind to the cat.   **e.** aren't
6. _d_ I guess the cat and mouse were not meant to live happily ever after.   **f.** haven't

156

Lesson 3.10 Contractions with **Not**

Rewrite It

Circle the two words in each sentence you could combine to make a contraction. Then, write the sentences using contractions.

1. Mr. Irving Mouse (can not) come out during the day.
   Mr. Irving Mouse can't come out during the day.

2. He (does not) want to run into Miss Lola Cat.
   He doesn't want to run into Miss Lola Cat.

3. Being chased (is not) Irving's idea of a good time.
   Being chased isn't Irving's idea of a good time.

4. He (did not) think Lola would be so rude.
   He didn't think Lola would be so rude.

5. They (are not) going to be able to share this house.
   They aren't going to be able to share this house.

Try It

1. Write a sentence using one of the following pairs of words: **is not, are not, did not,** or **have not**
   Answers will vary.

2. Now, rewrite your sentence using a contraction.
   Answers will vary.

157

Language Arts Grade 2 Answers

NAME _____

Lesson 3.11 Contractions with **Am, Is, Are**

Some contractions are formed with the words **am**, **is**, and **are**. The apostrophe takes the place of the letter **a** in **am**. It takes the place of **i** in **is**. It takes the place of **a** in **are**.

I am = I'm
we are = we're
it is = it's
she is = she's

you are = you're
they are = they're
he is = he's

Proof It

Read the diary entry below. Draw a line through the words in bold type. Then, write the contractions above the words.

Dear Diary,

~~I'm~~
~~I am~~ going to my karate class on Saturday morning. ~~It is~~ a It's

class for beginners. Maria and Toby are taking karate, too. ~~They~~ They're

~~are~~ in my class. Maria learned some karate moves from her

older brother. ~~He is~~ in a different class. Maria knows how to do He's

more kicks than anyone else. I think ~~she is~~ the best student. Allan she's

is our karate teacher. ~~He is~~ 39 years old. He has been doing He's

karate since he was five. He has a black belt. Maria, Toby, and

I plan to take lessons for a long time. ~~We are~~ going to get our We're

black belts one day, too.

158

NAME _____

Lesson 3.11 Contractions with **Am, Is, Are**

Complete It

Fill in the blanks below with a contraction from the box.

| It's | You're | He's |
| We're | She's | They're |

1. I think Allan is a great teacher. He's patient and funny.

2. Maria's mom comes to every class. She's interested in what we learn.

3. Toby and Maria are cousins. They're both part of the Tarrano family.

4. Maria, Toby, and I will get our yellow belts next month. We're excited to move up a level.

5. I like karate class a lot. It's a good way to exercise and make friends.

6. Do you think you would like to try karate? You're welcome to come watch one of our classes.

Try It

1. Write a sentence using the contraction for **she is**.
   Answers will vary.

2. Write a sentence using the contraction for **they are**.
   Answers will vary.

159

NAME _____

Lesson 3.12 Contractions with **Will**

Many contractions are formed with pronouns and the verb **will**. An apostrophe (') takes the place of the letters **wi** in **will**.

I will = I'll
you will = you'll
she will = she'll
he will = he'll

it will = it'll
we will = we'll
they will = they'll

Match It

Match each pair of underlined words with its contraction. Write the letter of the contraction in the space.

1. c I will travel into space one day.   a. She'll

2. f A spaceship will take me there. It will move very fast.   b. We'll

3. e You will be my co-pilot.   c. I'll

4. a My sister, Eva, can come along, too. She will direct the spaceship.   d. They'll

5. b We will make many important discoveries.   e. You'll

6. d Our families can have a party when we return. They will be so proud!   f. It'll

160

NAME _____

Lesson 3.12 Contractions with **Will**

Proof It

Read the newspaper article below. Draw a line through the underlined words. Then, write the contractions above the words.

Hughes to Become Youngest Astronaut

Jasmine Hughes is only nine years old. ~~She will~~ be the first child to She'll journey into space. Jasmine has been training since she was four. ~~She will~~ travel on the spaceship She'll Investigator. Six other astronauts will be in her crew. ~~They will~~ They'll have to work well as a

team. Darren Unger will be the commander. ~~He will~~ be the leader He'll of the crew. They know their mission is important. ~~It will~~ help It'll scientists learn more about the universe. The world will be able to watch parts of the trip on TV. ~~We will~~ see history being made! We'll

Try It

1. Write a sentence using the contraction for **he will**.
   Answers will vary.

2. Write a sentence using the contraction for **I will**.
   Answers will vary.

161

Spectrum Grade 2
300

Language Arts Grade 2 Answers

NAME_____

Lesson 3.13 Plural Nouns with **s**

The word **plural** means **more than one**. To make most nouns plural, just add **s**.

one clock → two clock**s**   one shirt → three shirt**s**

one girl → many girl**s**   one squirrel → six squirrel**s**

Complete It

Read the sentences below. Complete each sentence with the plural form of the word in parentheses ( ).

Example: The ____boys____ played tag until it got dark outside. (boy)

1. There are five blue ____stripes____ on Greece's flag. (stripe)

2. China's flag has five ____stars____. (star)

3. The two ____colors____ in Denmark's flag are red and white. (color)

4. Some flags have small ____pictures____ on them. (picture)

5. Jamaica's flag has four ____triangles____. (triangle)

6. ____Moons____ are on the flags of many countries. (Moon)

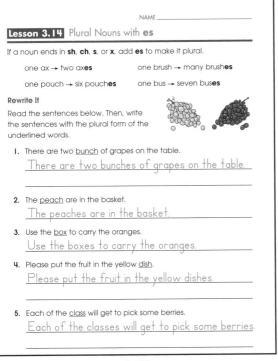

162

NAME_____

Lesson 3.13 Plural Nouns with **s**

Solve It

The words below are all things that are on state flags of the United States. Write the plural form of each word on the line. Then, fill in the crossword puzzle using the numbers and the plural clues.

Down

1. date ____dates____

2. bird ____birds____

3. flower ____flowers____

5. tree ____trees____

Across

4. animal ____animals____

6. word ____words____

7. star ____stars____

Crossword:
- d a t e s
- b i r d s
- f l o w e r s
- a n i m a l s
- w o r d s
- s t a r s

Try It

Write two sentences below. Use the plural form of at least one word from the box in each sentence.

paint	pencil	paintbrush
book	folder	pen
crayon	notebook	color

1. ____Answers will vary.____

2. ____Answers will vary.____

163

NAME_____

Lesson 3.14 Plural Nouns with **es**

If a noun ends in **sh**, **ch**, **s**, or **x**, add **es** to make it plural.

one ax → two ax**es**   one brush → many brush**es**

one pouch → six pouch**es**   one bus → seven bus**es**

Rewrite It

Read the sentences below. Then, write the sentences with the plural form of the underlined words.

1. There are two bunch of grapes on the table.

   ____There are two bunches of grapes on the table.____

2. The peach are in the basket.

   ____The peaches are in the basket.____

3. Use the box to carry the oranges.

   ____Use the boxes to carry the oranges.____

4. Please put the fruit in the yellow dish.

   ____Please put the fruit in the yellow dishes.____

5. Each of the class will get to pick some berries.

   ____Each of the classes will get to pick some berries.____

164

NAME_____

Lesson 3.14 Plural Nouns with **es**

Proof It

Read the paragraphs below. The underlined words should be plural. To make a word plural, make a caret (^) at the end of the word. Then, write the letter or letters you want to add above the caret.

Example: There are three **watch**^es in the glass case.

We waited on the bench^es outside the school. The bus^es picked us up at nine o'clock. We went to Sunnyvale Apple Orchard. Mr. Krup gave us some box^es to use. He showed us how to pick ripe apples. Many branch^es were heavy with fruit. There were also some blueberry bush^es on the farm.

When we were done picking, the tractor brought us back to the farmhouse. We ate our lunch^es at some picnic tables. Mrs. Krup gave us glass^es of lemonade. Tomorrow, we'll make apple pies.

Try It

Write two sentences below. Use the plural form of at least one word from the box in each sentence.

| fox | watch |
| beach | brush |

1. ____Answers will vary.____

2. ____Answers will vary.____

165

Language Arts Grade 2 Answers

NAME_____

Lesson 3.15 Irregular Plural Nouns

Some plural nouns do not follow the rules you have learned. To form the plurals of these nouns, do not add **s** or **es**. Instead, the whole word changes. Here are some examples.

one **man** → three **men**   one **foot** → two **feet**
one **woman** → eight **women**   one **goose** → four **geese**
one **child** → a few **children**   one **tooth** → many **teeth**
one **mouse** → twenty **mice**

Some nouns do not change at all in their plural forms.

one **deer** → many **deer**   one **moose** → nine **moose**
one **fish** → sixty **fish**   one **sheep** → one hundred **sheep**

Match It

Read the phrases in Column 1. Then, draw a line to match each phrase to its plural in Column 2.

Column 1   Column 2

one tooth   nine deer
one child   four feet
one foot   twelve mice
one goose   several teeth
one deer   lots of children
one mouse   two men
one man   seven geese

166

NAME_____

Lesson 3.15 Irregular Plural Nouns

Solve It

Write the plural form of each word on the line. Then, see if you can find each plural word in the word search puzzle. Circle the words you find in the puzzle. Words can be found across and down.

1. woman ___women___
2. fish ___fish___
3. moose ___moose___
4. mouse ___mice___
5. foot ___feet___
6. sheep ___sheep___
7. child ___children___
8. tooth ___teeth___

n	l	m	i	h	l	f	g	c	q
c	h	i	l	d	r	e	n	b	u
n	t	c	t	l	w	e	i	h	x
s	h	e	e	p	o	t	v	k	m
f	s	a	e	k	m	o	o	s	e
e	r	h	t	g	e	d	f	z	p
f	i	s	h	j	n	p	u	g	j

Try It

Write two sentences below. Use the plural form of at least one word from the box in each sentence.

foot	mouse
man	deer
fish	goose

1. _Answers will vary._
2. _Answers will vary._

167

NAME_____

Lesson 3.16 Pronouns **I** and **Me**

I and **me** are both pronouns. **Pronouns** are words that take the places of nouns. The pronouns **I** and **me** are used when the writer is talking about himself or herself.

I took the bus downtown. **I** bought a sandwich. The police officer waved to **me**. **I** walked to the museum. The woman behind the desk gave **me** a ticket.

When you are talking about yourself and another person, always put the other person first.

Robyn and I left early.
He gave the shells to **Dexter and me**.

Complete It

Complete each sentence below with the pronoun **I** or **me**. Write the pronoun in the space.

1. ___I___ was born in New York in 1899.
2. My five brothers and sisters were older than ___me___.
3. My wife and ___I___ moved to a farm in Maine.
4. ___I___ loved to read, write, and do chores on the farm.
5. A spider in my barn gave ___me___ the idea for a children's story.

Do you know who the mystery person is? It is E. B. White, the famous author of the books <u>Charlotte's Web</u> and <u>Stuart Little</u>.

168

NAME_____

Lesson 3.16 Pronouns **I** and **Me**

Proof It

Read the sentences below. If the correct pronoun is used, put a check mark on the line. If it is not, write the correct pronoun on the line.

1. _I_ Me went to the store yesterday.
2. _✓_ Chris and I are on the same baseball team.
3. _me_ Is that package for I?
4. _I_ My sister and me are going to the playground.
5. _✓_ I had a great time last year at the museum.
6. _me_ Running is good for I.
7. _I_ Dad and me took the subway downtown.
8. _me_ Amina gave I an invitation to the party.

Try It

On the lines below, write two sentences about things that happened to you last week. Use **I** in one sentence, and **me** in the other.

1. _Answers will vary._
2. _Answers will vary._

169

Language Arts Grade 2 Answers

Lesson 3.17 Comparative Adjectives

Adjectives are words that describe nouns. They give the reader more information. Add **er** to an adjective to show that one thing is more than something else. Add **est** to an adjective to show that it is the most.

Rosa is tall.   Jill is tall**er**.   Bethany is tall**est**.

Identify It

Read the sentences below. Circle the correct adjective in parentheses.

1. Mount Everest is the (highest, higher) mountain.
2. The (tall, tallest) waterfall in the world is Angel Falls in Venezuela.
3. The Nile River is (longest, longer) than the Amazon River.
4. The Pacific Ocean is (deeper, deep) than the Indian Ocean.
5. It is the world's (deeper, deepest) ocean.

170

Lesson 3.17 Comparative Adjectives

Complete It

Fill in the spaces with the missing adjectives.

young	younger	youngest
fast	faster	fastest
dark	darker	darkest
hard	harder	hardest
new	newer	newest
short	shorter	shortest
small	smaller	smallest
kind	kinder	kindest

Try It

On the lines below, write two sentences. Your sentences should compare people or things that are alike in some way.

Example: Stacey is older than Hasaan.   Val is the oldest.

1. Answers will vary.
2. Answers will vary.

171

Lesson 3.18 Synonyms

Synonyms are words that have the same, or almost the same, meanings. Synonyms can help you become a better writer. They make your writing more interesting to read. Here are some examples of synonyms.

little, tiny, small   easy, simple

begin, start   quick, fast

under, below   laugh, giggle

Match It

Match each word in the first column with its synonym in the second column. Write the letter of the synonym on the line.

1. _g_ beautiful   a. enjoy
2. _d_ boat   b. toss
3. _a_ like   c. happy
4. _f_ tired   d. ship
5. _h_ grin   e. pal
6. _c_ glad   f. sleepy
7. _e_ friend   g. pretty
8. _b_ throw   h. smile

172

Lesson 3.18 Synonyms

Complete It

Read the sentences below. Each underlined word has a synonym in the box. Write the synonym on the line at the end of the sentence.

| giggled | bugs | hop |
| dad | pick | liked | terrific |

1. Malik needed to choose a topic for his report. ___pick___
2. He and his father sat down at the computer. ___dad___
3. Malik enjoyed using the Internet for school projects. ___liked___
4. All of a sudden, he had a great idea. ___terrific___
5. "I think I'm going to do my report on insects," Malik told his dad. ___bugs___
6. Malik and Dad watched a cartoon cricket jump across the computer screen. ___hop___
7. Malik laughed when the cricket stopped and waved. ___giggled___

Try It

1. Write a sentence using a synonym for the word **small**.
   Answers will vary.
2. Write a sentence using a synonym for the word **yelled**.
   Answers will vary.

173

Spectrum Grade 2
303

Language Arts Grade 2 Answers

NAME

Lesson 3.19 Antonyms

An **antonym** is a word that means the opposite of another word. Here are some examples of antonyms.

big, little old, young

happy, sad first, last

right, wrong never, always

Identify It

There are two antonyms in each sentence below. Circle each pair of antonyms.

1. The tall bottle is next to the short can.

2. Kent wore his new shirt with his favorite pair of old jeans.

3. I thought the quiz would be hard but it was easy.

4. Did Miranda smile or frown when she saw you?

5. One pair of shoes is too tight and one pair is too loose.

6. Open the cupboard, take out the cereal, and close the door.

7. It was hot outside, but it will be cold tomorrow.

8. Stephen was the first person in line and the last person to leave.

9. Would you rather go in the morning or night?

174

NAME

Lesson 3.19 Antonyms

Solve It

In the spaces, write an antonym for each word below. Then, circle the antonyms in the word search puzzle. Words can be found across and down.

1. yell w h i s p e r
2. pull p u s h
3. empty f u l l
4. win l o s e
5. yes n o
6. love h a t e
7. over u n d e r
8. down u p

q	a	w	h	i	s	p	e	r	p
f	u	l	l	c	g	u	p	j	t
m	n	n	o	k	h	s	p	x	a
a	d	g	s	y	b	h	a	t	e
z	e	b	e	o	l	p	f	d	j
d	r	l	c	h	z	k	p	l	o

Try It

1. Write a sentence using an antonym for **loud**.

Answers will vary.

2. Write a sentence using an antonym for **soft**.

Answers will vary.

175

NAME

Lesson 3.20 Homophones

Homophones are words that sound alike but have different spellings and meanings. Here are some examples of homophones.

to = toward We went **to** the gym.
OR
use **to** with a verb Dennis wants **to** skate.
two = the number that Give the dog **two** biscuits.
comes after one

too = also We will go, **too**.
OR
too = very; more than enough Lindy is **too** young to go.

by = next to The bag is **by** the door.
bye = good-bye Karim waved and said **bye**.
buy = to purchase something I will **buy** three pears.

right = the opposite of wrong That is the **right** answer.
write = to record your words **Write** a report about the book.

Complete It

Choose the correct word to complete each sentence. Write it on the line.

1. I would like ___to___ see *Pinocchio* on ice. (to, too)

2. My sister wants to go, ___too___. (two, too)

3. Mom said she will try to ___buy___ tickets tonight. (bye, buy)

4. I am going to ___write___ about the show in my diary. (write, right)

176

NAME

Lesson 3.20 Homophones

Proof It

Read the poster below. There are five mistakes. Cross out each mistake. Then, write the correct homophone above it.

> Come see Pinocchio on ice!
> too
> This show is ~~to~~ much fun to miss.
> right
> Make the ~~write~~ choice, and you'll be glad you
> to
> came ~~two~~ see these skaters.
> by
> The ice rink is downtown ~~buy~~ the theater.
> Buy
> ~~By~~ two tickets and get one free!
>
> March 10—March 15

Try It

1. Write a sentence using the word **too**.

Answers will vary.

2. Write a sentence using the word **buy**.

Answers will vary.

3. Write a sentence using the word **write**.

Answers will vary.

177

Language Arts Grade 2 Answers

NAME _____

Lesson 3.21 Multiple-Meaning Words

Multiple-meaning words are words that are spelled the same but have different meanings. You have to read the sentence carefully to know which meaning a writer wants to use.

Casey got a baseball **bat** and a mitt for his birthday.
(a wooden stick used in baseball)
The brown **bat** eats about 2,000 insects a night.
(a small, flying mammal)

There is a swing set and a jungle gym at the **park**.
(an open, grassy area for relaxing)
Park next to the green van. (to stop and leave a car)

Find It

Read this dictionary entry. It shows two different meanings for the same word. Each meaning is a different part of speech. Use the dictionary entry to answer the questions below.

cold *adj.* having a low temperature; cool, chilly, or icy; not warm; *noun* an illness that often includes a cough, a sore throat, and a runny nose

1. It will be cold but sunny on Saturday.
   Which definition of **cold** is used in this sentence? __a__
   a. the first definition   **b.** the second definition

2. Destiny caught a cold from her brother.
   Which definition of **cold** is used in this sentence? __b__
   a. the first definition   **b.** the second definition

178

NAME _____

Lesson 3.21 Multiple-Meaning Words

Match It

Look at the definitions of the underlined word. Choose the definition that matches the way the word is used. Write the letter of that definition on the line.

1. __b__ Airplanes <u>fly</u> at amazing speeds.
   a. a small insect with two wings
   b. to move through the air

2. __a__ The <u>leaves</u> were red, gold, and brown.
   a. parts of a tree or a plant   **b.** goes away

3. __b__ May I <u>pet</u> your cat?
   a. an animal that lives with people
   b. to touch lightly or stroke

4. __a__ The Krugers did not <u>watch</u> the entire movie.
   a. view or look at   **b.** a small clock worn on the wrist

5. __a__ Keely will <u>train</u> her puppy to roll over.
   a. to teach something by doing it over and over
   b. a long line of cars that run on a track

Try It

The word **fair** can have two meanings: **equal** or **a place**, **like a carnival, where there are rides and games**. Write two sentences using the word **fair**. It should have a different meaning in each sentence.

1. Answers will vary. _____
2. Answers will vary. _____

179

Reading Grade 2 Answers

---

1. What kinds of bridges does Dad build?

heavy, strong ones and light ones

2. Why is Dad nervous?

It is his first day at a new job.

3. How does the boy know that Dad is nervous?

He almost poured milk in his juice.

4. What kind of bridge did the boy and Dad make at home?

They filled the boy's room with bridges from boxes, blocks and pans.

5. From whose point of view is the story told?

the boy

6. The last line of the story says that Dad is going to make one more bridge at home. What does he use to make it?

things on the breakfast table

7. Is the first sentence of the story a fact or an opinion?

an opinion

191

---

1. This passage is mostly about

_____ old bridges.

___X___ kinds of bridges.

_____ making bridges.

2. The author wrote this selection to

_____ make you laugh.   ___X___ help you learn.

3. Think about what you already know about bridges. What are bridges for? to get across or to get over something; to carry things across

4. This passage tells about another use for bridges. What is it?

Some bridges were made to carry water.

5. Are all bridges made by humans? What might a natural bridge be made of?

No. Possible answer: A natural bridge could be made of rocks or a log.

6. How are bridges with arches and beams different?

Bridges with arches have curved supports. Bridges with beams have straight supports.

7. *The Golden Gate Bridge is the prettiest bridge in the U.S.* Is this a fact or an opinion?

an opinion

193

---

1. How does the text help you understand how long a 24-mile-long bridge is?

It takes half an hour to go across.

2. How does the text help you understand how high the bridge in Colorado is?

It says that a 75-story building could fit under the bridge.

3. If you do not like to look over the side of a bridge, why would the bridge in Australia be a good one to cross?

because it is very wide

4. Why is the bridge in India a bridge to remember?

It is a very busy bridge, with cars and trucks and walking traffic.

5. Name three things, other than cars, that cross bridges in the selection.

Possible answers: trucks, trains, bikes, walkers

6. What do some people do if they are nervous on a bridge?

They hold their breath until they get to the other side.

195

---

1. What do Mom and Emily worry about?

They worry that their stuff will be squished.

2. Circle the word that best tells how Emily feels about her stuffed animals.

hopeless   (caring)   harsh

3. What word best tells how Mom feels? Circle it.

relaxed   (worried)   careless

4. How do you think Dad feels about moving day?

Dad seems kind of excited.

5. What clues in the story help you know how Dad feels?

He says it has been a "good day's work."

6. How do you think Emily will feel when the move is complete? Explain.

Answers will vary.

7. Why did Emily put holes in one of the boxes?

so her stuffed animals could breathe

8. How does the picture on page 196 add to your understanding of the story?

Answers will vary.

197

Reading Grade 2 Answers

NAME _____

I. Why was Emily happy to go turn on the lights?

She wanted to check out the new house.

2. How did the picture make Emily feel?

It made her feel good, even though she missed her old house.

3. How did Emily feel about her new house?

She seems a little sad. Maybe she doesn't feel at home yet.

4. Write **I**, **2**, and **3** by these sentences to show what happened first, next, and last.

__1__ Emily turned on the lights.

__3__ Mom and Emily put a picture on the refrigerator.

__2__ Mom and Emily unpacked a box.

5. How would you feel about moving to a new home? Why?

Answers will vary.

6. Do you think Emily's mom understands how Emily feels? Explain.

Possible answer: Yes, Mom is trying to make Emily feel at home.

199

NAME _____

I. This story is mostly about

__X__ Emily's new room.

_____ how busy Mom is.

_____ Emily's toys.

2. At the beginning of the story, what does Emily think about her new room?

She doesn't like it. It is just plain white.

3. What does Emily think of her room at the end of the story?

She thinks it is just right.

4. What happened to change Emily's feelings?

She put her books in place and Mom made her bed.

5. How does Emily organize her books?

by size

6. How does Mom help Emily with her room?

She makes up Emily's bed for her.

7. What do you think Emily will do next in the story? Make a check mark next to your answer.

_____ Go on a bike ride

__✓__ Unpack more things in her room

_____ Call her grandma

201

NAME _____

Look at each picture and circle the sentence that goes with it.

I (Emily is eating breakfast.)

Emily is making her bed.

2. Dad is carrying a box.

(Dad is unpacking a box.)

3. What meal is the family eating?

breakfast

4. Why can't the family leave right away?

Emily is not dressed yet.

5. What is the setting for this story?

Emily's kitchen

6. Read each sentence. If it is a fact, write **F** on the line. If it is an opinion, write **O**.

__O__ San Antonio is an exciting place.

__F__ Mom and Emily laughed and raised their hands high.

__F__ We can ride in a river taxi.

203

NAME _____

I. What did you already know about Texas?

Answers will vary.

2. List two new things you learned about Texas.

Answers will vary.

3. What question would you like to ask about Texas?

Answers will vary.

4. Why do you think the author wrote this article about Texas?

__X__ to help the reader learn something

_____ to make the reader laugh

5. How do the boldface headings help organize the text?

Possible answer: They tell you where to find things in the text.

6. What are two things you learned from the illustrations that are not in the text?

Possible answers: Texas is called the Lone Star state. The state bird is the mockingbird.

7. Complete the sentence: Texas is number two both in

size; number of people living there

205

207

NAME _____

Write each word in the correct blank.

city	hotels	concert	ride

1. If you like music, go to a _____concert_____.
2. San Antonio is a large, modern _____city_____.
3. If you are tired, _____ride_____ in a river taxi.
4. People sleep in _____hotels_____ along the River Walk.
5. Which word best describes the city of San Antonio?

_____ rundown

__X__ beautiful

_____ cold

6. If you visited San Antonio, what would you most like to do?

Answers will vary.

7. What do you think a river taxi is?

Possible answer: A boat that charges money for a ride down the river.

209

NAME _____

1. How did Paul solve the problem with the holes?

He ended up crying, and his tears filled up the holes and made lakes.

2. Why did Babe run away?

He was upset about the holes he and Paul had made.

3. What made Babe come back?

He heard the people thanking Paul for the lakes.

4. People who tell tall tales stretch the truth. List one idea from the story that can't be true.

Ex: Paul's tears making rivers; Paul looking under river.

5. What is the story's setting? Minnesota

6. Why did the people of Minnesota thank Paul?

Paul's tears filled up all the holes his footprints had made.

7. What causes Paul Bunyan to cry?

Paul could not find Babe.

8. Who is the main character in the story?

Paul Bunyan

211

NAME _____

1. This story is mostly about

_____ how to draw.

__X__ Matt and Mom drawing.

_____ choosing colors.

Circle the best answer.

2. What do you think Mom and Matt will do next?

get ready for bed   go to school   (have a snack)

3. Write 1, 2, and 3 in the spaces below to show in what order events happened.

__2__ Mom shows Matt her flower.

__3__ Mom says she is hungry.

__1__ Matt says he is drawing a turtle.

4. There is a lot of dialogue in the story. Write one example of dialogue on the line. Tell how you know that it is dialogue.

Possible answer: "May I have the green, please?" It is in quotes.

5. At the end of the story, do you think Mom will really draw cheese? Why or why not?

Answers will vary.

6. What does drawing a turtle make Matt think of?

It makes him remember the turtle he saw by the road.

213

NAME _____

1. What is the author's purpose in writing this piece?

_____ to entertain

__X__ to teach

_____ to persuade

2. What can we learn from new art?

Possible answer: It helps us see the world in different ways and makes us ask questions.

3. What can we learn from old art?

We can learn about the people who made it long ago.

4. Tell in your own words what an art museum is.

Ex.: An art museum is a place where people take care of art and show it to other people.

5. Name two ways that art museums can be different from each other.

Some are big and famous. Some are small and not well known.

6. In the first paragraph, the text says that you can see art all around you. What art can you see right now?

Answers will vary.

7. If you visited an art museum, what kind of art would you hope to see?

Answers will vary.

Reading Grade 2 Answers

NAME _____

I. Why does Carly's face turn red the first time?

She drops her fork; Mr. Mendez is beside her.

2. Why couldn't Mrs. Mendez come to dinner?

She had to stay at work.

3. Based on your reading of the story, where do you think Mrs. Mendez works?

at an animal shelter

4. Why does Carly's face turn red the second time?

Carly speaks out a little too loudly at the table.

Circle the best answer.

5. What do you think will happen next?

Mrs. Mendez will arrive.   (Carly will ask for a kitten.)

Carly's cat will enter the room.

6. Write **T** for *true* or **F** for *false* next to each sentence below.

T Carly's dad works with Mr. Mendez.

F Carly's family has three cats.

T When Carly is embarrassed, her face turns red.

T The animal shelter is busy in the spring.

7. Why is the animal shelter extra busy in spring?

Many kittens are born in the spring.

215

NAME _____

I. This story is mostly about

_____ cats and dogs as pets.

__X__ a girl who wants a kitten.

_____ doing chores at home.

2. Carly thinks getting a cat is a good idea. What reasons does she give?

The animal shelter has too many; The Hamlins have one in their apartment.

3. What reason does Mom give for not getting a pet?

The apartment is too small.

4. What would you do if you were Carly?

Ex.: I would tell my parents I could take care of a cat all by myself.

5. Look at the last line of the first paragraph. The words *too many kittens* are in italics. Why do you think the author used italics here?

Possible answer: That part of the sentence is very important to Carly.

6. In paragraph 5, Carly *objects* to what her mom says. What does it mean to object?

to not agree

7. At the end of the story, why does Carly offer to help her parents think about getting a cat?

Possible answer: She wants to try to get them to agree with her.

217

NAME _____

I. The author wrote "Cats Long Ago" mostly to

__X__ give information.

_____ make you laugh.

2. Compare what you know about cats in Egypt with what you know about cats today. One idea is written for you.

In Egypt cats were respected

cats ate mice and rats; family shaved eyebrows when a cat died

Today cats are usually well cared for

cats eat mice and rats sometimes; family may be sad when a cat dies

3. What is one difference between us and the people in Egypt long ago?

Ex.: Many people like cats, but we don't really respect them.

4. What did Egyptians do when a family cat died?

They shaved their eyebrows.

5. How were cats helpful to Egyptians long ago?

They ate the mice and rats that ate the grain.

Use the text to fill in the blank in each sentence below.

6. Rats and mice ate the _____grain_____ that Egyptians stored.

7. Cats were the most _____respected_____ animals in Egypt.

8. Cats helped to _____protect_____ the grain.

219

NAME _____

I. This article is mostly about

_____ cats in animal shelters.

_____ how cute kittens are.

__X__ daily cat care.

2. After reading the article, do you think you could care for a cat? Why or why not?

Ex.: I think I could because I would feed and water it every day.

3. Write one idea that you find under each heading.

Food Ex.: Fill dish once a day.

Water Ex.: Give fresh water twice a day.

Other Needs Ex.: Clean litter box almost every day.

4. Why do you think the author used headings in this article?

Ex.: The headings make it easy to find information.

5. Read each sentence. Write **F** if it is a fact and **O** if it is an opinion.

F A cat needs to be fed every day.

O Cats make the best pets!

F If you have an indoor cat, it needs a litter box.

O If you adopt a cat, you should choose an older cat.

6. How often does a litter box need to be cleaned?

about every day

221

Reading Grade 2 Answers

NAME _____

1. What do cats do for themselves?

They bathe themselves several times a day.

2. What should a cat owner do once a year?

Take the cat to the vet.

3. Why might a long-haired cat need to be brushed more often than a short-haired cat?

It would take more work to keep the coat neat and clean.

4. If you had a cat, would you rather have a short-haired cat or a long-haired cat? Write why.

Answers will vary.

5. Why do cats need to have an operation?

so that they don't have more kittens

6. The text says that cats have rough tongues. How do you think this is helpful when they groom themselves?

Possible answer: It helps them remove loose fur.

7. Is it important to be a responsible cat owner? Explain.

Answers will vary.

223

NAME _____

1. At the beginning of the story, what did you predict would happen at the end?

Answers will vary.

2. Why does Carly worry when Dad speaks first?

Dad usually gives the bad news.

3. Have you ever wanted something as much as Carly wants a kitten? Tell about it.

Answers will vary.

4. In the story, who is Mitch?

_____ Carly's dad ___X___ Carly's brother _____ Carly's cousin

5. Why do you think Carly's parents want an older cat and not a kitten?

Possible answer: It will be calmer and easier to care for.

6. Do you think Carly will be happy about her parents' decision? Why or why not?

Answers will vary.

7. Look at the picture on page 224. What does the art add to the story? How do the kids looks like they are feeling?

Answers will vary.

8. Read the last line of the story again. What do you predict will happen next?

Possible answer: The kids will go with their parents to pick out a cat.

225

NAME _____

1. This story is mostly about

___X___ choosing a cat.

_____ Mr. Mendez's work.

_____ kittens who need homes.

2. Why didn't Carly choose the big black cat?

It hissed and batted at her hand; it wasn't friendly.

3. How did Mitch and Carly choose the gray cat?

It was friendly; it rubbed against their ankles.

4. What does it mean when a cat hisses at you?

Possible answer: It does not feel friendly.

5. Mrs. Mendez comes up in an earlier story. How does Carly's family know her?

Possible answer: She works at an animal shelter. Mr. Mendez works with Carly's dad.

6. Why does Mrs. Mendez think a grown-up cat is a good choice for a first pet?

It's a little easier than having a kitten.

7. What is the setting for this story?

an animal shelter

8. Do you think the Blake family will be good pet owners? Why or why not?

Answers will vary.

227

NAME _____

1. Which sentence best tells how Carly feels about today?

___X___ She is excited.

_____ She is worried.

2. What words or ideas in the story helped you answer question 1?

Ex.: She wondered what was special; she threw back the covers.

3. Where did Carly and Mitch look first for Mouse?

They looked under Carly's bed.

4. In what room did Carly find Mouse?

in the living room

5. Why was Mouse sleeping there?

He liked the sunshine.

6. Why do Carly and Mitch name their cat Mouse?

He is gray and made a little mewing noise.

7. Why is the title of the story funny?

Possible answer: It sounds like the story is about a mouse, but it is about a cat.

8. How do you think Carly feels about her new cat?

Answers will vary.

229

Reading Grade 2 Answers

---

1. Why was there a picnic on the baseball field?

It was the last day of school.

2. Why did everyone have to dash into the school?

because it started to rain

3. Why is Kyle's family taking care of Sparky?

because his grandparents are on a camping trip

4. Why does Sparky leave the room when Snowy comes in?

because he is afraid of the cat

5. What kind of animal is Sparky? How do you know?

a dog; Possible answer: In the picture, there is a dog in Kyle's room.

6. Think of what you learned about Kyle by reading his letter. Write three words you could use to describe him.

Possible answers: kind, helpful, friendly

7. In what time of year does the story take place?

_____ winter   _____ fall   __X__ summer

8. What clues in the text helped you answer number 7?

Possible answers: School is out. The garden is looking good.

231

---

1. Where did Kyle's grandparents go on their trip?

Mammoth Cave State Park

2. Why did they go there?

They like to look at rocks.

3. What did you learn about Kyle's grandparents by reading their letter?

Ex: They like to camp; they like rocks; they like hiking; they are in good health.

4. Where do Grandma and Grandpa live? in Ohio

5. Read each sentence. Write **F** if it is a fact and **O** if it is an opinion.

__O__ You and your parents would like it, too.

__O__ Our camping trip was wonderful!

__F__ We were underground for more than two miles.

__F__ Each day, we chose a different cave.

6. Based on their letter, you know that Grandma and Grandpa probably

_____ live in Kentucky.

__X__ like to have adventures.

_____ have several dogs.

7. What is the purpose of Grandma and Grandpa's letter?

Possible answer: to tell about their trip; to tell when they will come get Sparky

233

---

1. This article is mostly about

_____ how caves are formed.

__X__ the sights in Mammoth Cave.

_____ animals that live in caves.

2. What is special about Mammoth Cave?

Ex: It is the longest cave system in the world; it has 350 miles of passages.

3. Why might a fish that lives in a cave not have any eyes?

Ex: It is so dark, it wouldn't be able to see anyway.

4. If you went to Mammoth Cave, what would you most like to see? Write why.

Answers will vary.

5. Name two types of animals that are likely to live in Mammoth Cave.

Possible answer: bats, fish

6. Based on the article, how do you think the author feels about Mammoth Cave?

Possible answer: The author thinks it is a very interesting place.

7. How long do you think humans have known about the cave?

Possible answer: for at least 4,000 years

8. Why are the caves still a mystery to scientists?

There are hundreds of miles that probably haven't been found yet.

235

---

1. Write **1**, **2**, and **3** by these sentences to show what happened first, next, and last.

__2__ Dad stirred the paint.

__1__ Michelle got the radio.

__3__ Dad and Michelle painted.

2. What does Michelle have to do on each post?

Paint the front, then the edge, then the other edge.

3. Why does Michelle think she will blow up?

Ex: There are so many posts to paint; she is tired or bored.

4. Have you ever done a task that went on and on and on? Write about it.

Answers will vary.

5. In the second paragraph, why does Dad look grim?

Possible answer: Dad is not looking forward to starting.

6. What does Dad's painting hat tell you about him?

Possible answer: He does a lot of painting projects.

7. What can you learn about the story from the picture? Choose something that you didn't learn from the text.

Possible answers: It's a nice day; Michelle wears glasses.

8. What does Dad send Michelle inside to do?

to get the radio

237

Reading Grade 2 Answers

NAME _____

Put each word in the right blank.

water	hair	milk

1. First, Danny spilled the _____milk_____.

2. Then, he had a problem with his _____hair_____.

3. Next, he got sprayed with _____water_____.

4. What did Danny look like when he sat down in his desk?
   Ex: His hair and shirt were wet; his shirt didn't match his pants.

5. Have you ever had a mixed up day? Write about it.
   Answers will vary.

6. In the first paragraph, it says "the milk jumped out of the jug." What does this mean?
   Possible answer: He spilled the milk.

7. How does Danny notice the problem with his hair and shirt?
   He sees himself in a store window.

8. Write **T** for *true* or **F** for *false* next to each sentence below.
   _T_ Mr. Torres is Danny's teacher.
   _F_ Danny spilled orange juice on the table.
   _F_ Danny's dad drove him to school.
   _T_ The water fountain sprays Danny's shirt.

239

NAME _____

1. Write **1**, **2**, **3**, and **4** by these sentences to show what happened first, second, third, and last.
   _2_ The girls painted the volcano.
   _1_ The friends made a volcano.
   _4_ Bubbles came up out of the volcano.
   _3_ Baking soda and vinegar went into the volcano.

Some of these sentences are about **real** things. Write **R** by them. The other sentences are about **make believe** things. Write **M** by them.

2. _M_ The girls can build a real volcano.
3. _M_ A real volcano can be on someone's back porch.
4. _R_ The girls do projects together.
5. _R_ Mothers help with projects.

6. A mixture of two things makes the volcano bubble up. What two things do the girls use?
   baking soda   _vinegar_

7. Who is Mrs. Metzer?
   the girls' teacher

8. Look at the picture. Why are the girls wearing goggles?
   to protect their eyes

9. Was the project a success? How do you know?
   Yes, the girls clap and say, "Yea, it worked!"

241

NAME _____

1. Who is coming to visit Lisa's family?
   her two cousins

2. Lisa's cousins won't be sleeping in her room. How does she feel about this? Why?
   Lisa is glad. She was worried there wouldn't be enough room in her bed.

3. What do you think will happen next in the story? Circle the correct answer.

   Lisa and her brother will go to bed.   Lisa will hide her dress-up clothes.

   (The cousins will arrive.)

4. Look at the picture. What is happening in the thought bubble over Lisa's head?
   Possible answer: Lisa is imagining how crowded her bed would be.

5. How does the picture help you to understand the story better?
   Possible answer: You can tell what Lisa is thinking.

Fill in the blank to complete each sentence below.

6. Lisa's cousins will be staying for _a week_.

7. Lisa doesn't want her stuffed animals to get _hurt_.

8. Mrs. Shaw says that the family will visit the _zoo_ one day.

9. The Shaws' extra bedroom is painted _green_.

10. Lisa's _cousins_ have visited before.

243

NAME _____

1. How does everyone feel about going to the zoo?
   _____ They are tired.   _X_ They are eager.

2. Why isn't Julia very interested in seeing the tigers?
   She doesn't like animals who could eat her.

3. Write **first**, **next**, and **last** on the lines to show the order in which events happened.
   last Lisa wants to see the zebras.
   first Mrs. Shaw asks if everyone is buckled in.
   next Julia makes a face.

4. What does Charlie say would happen if Julia were a mouse?
   an owl would eat her

5. How are Charlie and Julia related to each other?
   They are brother and sister.

6. Is this story realistic, or is it a fantasy? Explain.
   realistic; Possible answer: It tells about things that could happen in real life.

7. What animals would you like to see if you went to the zoo?
   Answers will vary.

8. What was the author's purpose in writing this story?
   _____ to entertain   _X_ to make you want to visit the zoo
   _____ to teach you about zoo animals

245

Reading Grade 2 Answers

NAME _____

1. What is a large group of zebras called?

a herd

2. Why does a herd move from place to place?

They eat grass, then move to a new place where there is more grass.

3. What are some other animals that move in groups?

antelopes, gnus, wildebeest

4. Why do zebras' stripes make it hard for lions to catch a zebra?

Ex: The stripes make the zebras blend together. The lion can't see just one zebra to chase.

5. How are a zebra's stripes similar to a human's fingerprints?

Both are one of a kind.

6. What animals are a threat to zebras?

lions

7. In what part of the world are zebras found?

in Africa

8. A zebra's stripes are a form of camouflage. What is another animal that uses camouflage? Explain.

Answers will vary.

247

NAME _____

1. In what three kinds of places do tigers live?

mountains, forests and wet, grassy areas

2. How are these places different?

Answers will vary.

3. How does the author help you with the word tigress?

The author wrote "mother tiger" first, then used the word "tigress."

4. Under what heading can you find information about when a tiger hunts?

How Tigers Live

5. What is similar about the way the articles on pages 246 and 248 are organized?

The headings are very similar.

6. In what kinds of places do tigers like to sleep?

They sleep in cool places, like caves or tall grasses.

7. Tigers hunt at night. What other kinds of animals hunt at night? Think of at least two examples.

Possible answers: raccoons, owls

8. Is this article fiction or nonfiction? How do you know?

nonfiction; The article contains facts about tigers. It is not a story.

249

NAME _____

1. Do you think owls would be able to live in a city? Explain.

Answers will vary.

2. What would happen if an owl made noise as it flew?

Ex: It would not be able to sneak up on its prey.

3. What do the three headings have in common?

They all name parts of an owl's body.

4. Why are an owl's feet important for hunting?

They can swoop down and catch their prey with their claws.

5. Why does the author say, "An owl flies on silent wings"?

They make no noise during flight.

6. Based on the text, what is prey?

Animals that are hunted by other animals.

7. Which two senses are most important to an owl for hunting?

seeing   hearing

8. Name three animals that owls eat.

Possible answers: mice, rats, rabbits

251

NAME _____

1. Why didn't Julia care for the sleeping tiger?

It was lying in the dirt.

2. Why does Lisa want stripes?

She wants stripes because she liked the zebras so much.

Some of these sentences are about **real** things. Write **R** by them. The other sentences are about **make believe** things. Write **M** by them.

3. M Animals ride in car seats.

4. R Children sleep in beds.

5. R People climb rocks.

6. M Girls perch in trees.

7. Why does Julia think that owls are wise?

They sleep high up where they are safe.

8. What do you think Charlie's favorite part of the zoo visit was?

He liked the tigers best.

9. What did the tiger do that the kids admired?

_____ roared   X climbed rocks   _____ slept

10. Do you think the kids will want to visit the zoo again? Why or why not?

Possible answer: Yes, because it seems like that had a great time.

253

Reading Grade 2 Answers

NAME _____

1. Which word best describes the boy's feelings about his grandparents?

(fond) excited hopeless

2. Why do you think the fort "got bigger" every time Gramps told the story?

Ex: He wanted to keep the story interesting, so he had to change it each time.

3. What do you think the boy might do next?

Answers will vary. Ex: He might build a fort with his dad.

4. Mark the sentence that is true.

___X___ Gramps grew up on a farm.

_____ Gramps grew up in the city.

5. What information in the story helped you answer question **4**?

Gramps and his brother had a barn with hay.

6. Who is telling the story?

_____ Gramps   ___X___ the boy   _____ the boy's dad

7. Read the two sentences below. Write **C** for *cause* next to one and **E** for *effect* next to the other.

___C___ Gram and Gramps have headed home.

___E___ Everything seems quiet now.

8. Why do you think Gram's face sometimes turns red?

She gets embarrassed when everyone sees her hum and dance.

255

NAME _____

1. Gina knows she will not be able to swim this afternoon because

she hears thunder   .

2. Mom frowned because she saw that it was raining.

3. This story is mostly about

_____ the rules for playing hopscotch.

_____ cleaning out a closet full of games.

___X___ how a girl and her mom spend an afternoon.

4. Why didn't Gina like her mom's ideas at first?

She thought they were little-kid games.

5. How did the afternoon turn out for Gina?

She thought it was pretty fun, even if they were little-kid games.

6. If the next day is sunny, what do you think Gina and her mom will do?

go swimming

7. What is the setting for this story?

Gina and Mom's house

8. What games do you like to play on rainy afternoons?

Answers will vary.

257

NAME _____

1. Write **1**, **2**, **3**, and **4** by these sentences to show the correct order of the steps in the water cycle.

___4___ Rain, snow, hail, or sleet falls to the ground.

___2___ Water vapor rises and forms clouds.

___1___ The sun's heat causes water to form water vapor.

___3___ Water drops form and become heavy.

2. Look at the picture of the water cycle. What do the arrows above the ocean tell you?

Ex: They show what direction the water is moving.

3. Explain the water cycle in your own words.

Answers will vary.

4. What happens when the water drops in a cloud get too heavy?

They fall to the ground as rain.

5. What rises up into the air to form clouds?

___X___ water vapor   _____ hail   _____ snow

6. Name three places you can find water in nature.

Possible answer: lakes, rivers, oceans

7. Here is an effect: **Water vapor rises into the air.** What is the cause?

Possible answer: Heat from the sun warms water.

259

NAME _____

1. Why does Gina's dad get excited about the corn?

because he knows it's fresh

2. Why isn't some of the fresh food really fresh?

It may have been picked days or weeks ago, then washed and trucked in to the store.

3. What does Gina's dad do that makes her laugh?

He made the corn look like ears on top of his head.

4. Where did you find the answer to question 3?

in the picture

5. Tell two things you know about Dad from reading the story.

Possible answers: He's funny; He cares about where food comes from.

6. What does Gina think about the corn after she eats it?

She thinks it's the best corn she's ever had.

7. Read each sentence. If it is a fact, write **F** on the line. If it is an opinion, write **O**.

___O___ It was the best corn I ever ate.

___O___ It's nice to see fresh food that was grown nearby.

___F___ We chose six ears.

261

Reading Grade 2 Answers

NAME _____

Write these steps in the correct order.

- watch plants grow
- plant seeds
- water soil
- harvest corn
- prepare soil

1. prepare soil
2. plant seeds
3. water soil
4. watch plants grow
5. harvest corn

6. At the end of the article, why does the author say, "Pass the butter and the salt, please"?

   It will be time to eat the corn.

7. What is the main idea of paragraph 2?

   You need to prepare the soil before you plant the corn.

8. It takes the seeds __10__ to __15__ days to sprout.

9. Based on the text, how do you think the author feels about growing corn?

   Possible answer: excited

10. If you could choose to grow something in a garden, what would it be? Why?

   Answers will vary.

263

NAME _____

1. Today, corn is used in thousands of products. How is that different from many years ago?

   It used to be eaten or fed to cattle and hogs.

2. The article mentions two food products that come from corn. What are they?

   corn syrup   corn starch

3. Half of the corn grown in America is fed to cattle and hogs. Why is that important?

   Answers will vary.

4. What are two ways to use corn, aside from eating it?

   Possible answers: laundry soap; fuel

5. What is the author's purpose for writing this article?

   _____ to get people to buy more corn

   __X__ to teach about the uses of corn

   _____ to make you laugh

6. **Corn is no longer fed to farm animals.** Is this true or false?

   false

7. Do you think ethanol is a good way to power cars? Why or why not?

   Answers will vary.

265

NAME _____

1. Explain how the Nolan Street picnic works.

   Everyone brings one dish of food. Then, you go along the table and wonder what to try.

2. Who do you think made the fruit pizza?

   Gina's dad

3. Which of these sentences best tells how Gina feels about food?

   _____ If it's food, I'll try it.

   _____ I like to try new foods.

   __X__ I'll try something only if I know what it is.

   _____ I like trying foods that have fruit in them.

4. Did Gina like the fruit pizza? How could you tell?

   She liked it. She asked for another piece, then asked for the recipe.

5. In paragraph 3, Gina says she took "safe things." What do you think she means by "safe"?

   Possible answer: Foods she had had before.

6. Who does Gina go to the picnic with?

   her parents

7. Do you enjoy trying new foods? Explain.

   Answers will vary.

267

NAME _____

Write these steps in the correct order. (Not all of the recipe's steps are here.)

- chill
- bake dough
- press dough into circle
- slice and arrange fruit
- make cream cheese mixture

1. press dough into circle
2. bake dough
3. make cream cheese mixture
4. slice and arrange fruit
5. chill

Recipes often use short forms of words called **abbreviations**. Match the abbreviations in the box with their common recipe words.

C.	oz.	tsp.	pkg.

6. teaspoon _____tsp._____

7. cup _____C._____

8. ounce _____oz._____

9. package _____pkg._____

10. What step do you have to do after you bake the pizza dough, before you add the spread?

   _____ arrange the fruit   __X__ cool it

   _____ cut it into wedges

269

Reading Grade 2 Answers

NAME _____

1. This story is mostly about

_____ a girl playing in the wet grass.

_____ how a rain storm hurt some plants.

__X__ two neighbor girls and how they meet.

2. What do you think will happen next in the story?

Answers will vary.

_____

Use the story to fill in the blanks and complete each sentence.

3. Roxie likes to grow __sunflowers__.

4. Yuki is looking at raindrops on the ____grass____.

5. Roxie and Yuki are on opposite sides of the ____fence____.

6. Yuki's mom has already met Roxie's ____mom____.

7. In what season do you think this story takes place? Explain your answer.

Possible answer: summer; Everything is green, and Roxie is growing flowers.

_____

8. What are two adjectives you could use to describe the grass in the yard?

Possible answers: shiny, sparkly

271

NAME _____

1. What did you think of when you read the title, "The Sunflower House"?

Answers will vary.

2. Was your idea anything like the sunflower house described in the directions? Explain.

Answers will vary.

3. What information is given only in the diagram?

The measurements of the circle and the ditch.

4. Would you have been able to follow the directions without the diagram? Explain.

Answers will vary.

5. Do sunflowers need a sunny or shady place to grow?

sunny

6. For which part will you probably need a grown-up's help?

digging a ditch around the string

7. How far apart should you plant the seeds?

nine inches

8. Why do you remove one seed before you cover the rest with dirt?

so you have an opening for the door

273